PHILIP ALLAN

LITERATURE GUIDE

FOR GCSE

AN INSPECTOR CALLS

J. B. PRIESTLEY

Najoud Ensaff

With thanks to Jeanette Weatherall for reviewing the manuscript of this book

Philip Allan Updates, an imprint of Hodder Education, an Hachette UK company, Market Place, Deddington, Oxfordshire OX15 0SE

Orders

Bookpoint Ltd, 130 Milton Park, Abingdon, Oxfordshire OX14 4SB
tel: 01235 827827
fax: 01235 400401
e-mail: education@bookpoint.co.uk
Lines are open 9.00 a.m.–5.00 p.m., Monday to Saturday, with a 24-hour message answering service. You can also order through the Philip Allan Updates website: www.philipallan.co.uk

P02014

Contents

Getting the most from this book and website

How to use this guide

You may find it useful to read sections of this guide when you need them, rather than reading it from start to finish. For example, you may find it helpful to read the *Context* section before you start reading the play, or to read the *Plot and structure* section in conjunction with the play — whether to back up your first reading of it at school or college or to help you revise. The sections relating to assessments will be especially useful in the weeks leading up to the exam.

The following features have been used throughout this guide:

● **What are the play's main themes?**

Target your thinking

A list of **introductory questions** to target your thinking is provided at the beginning of each chapter. Look back at these once you have read the chapter and check you have understood each of them before you move on.

Build critical skills

Broaden your thinking about the text by answering the questions in the **Pause for thought** boxes. They are intended to encourage you to consider your own opinions in order to develop your skills of criticism and analysis.

Pause for thought

Grade-boosting advice

Pay particular attention to the Grade booster boxes. Students with a firm grasp of these ideas are likely to be aiming for the top grades.

Grade *booster*

Key quotations are highlighted for you, and you may wish to use these as evidence in your examination answers. Page references are given for the Heinemann edition of the text (ISBN 978-0-435232-82-5). For example, a reference to H56, L12 means that a quotation appears on line 12 of page 56 in the Heinemann edition.

> **Key quotation**
>
> 'As if a girl of that sort would ever refuse money!'
> (Mrs Birling, H47, L1–2)

Be exam-ready

The **Grade focus** sections explain how you may be assessed and distinguish between higher and foundation responses.

Grade *focus*

Get the top grades

Use the **Text focus** boxes to practise evaluating the text in detail and looking for evidence to support your understanding.

Text **focus**

Develop evaluation skills

Review your learning

Use the **Review your learning** sections to test your knowledge after you have read each chapter. Answers to the questions are provided in the final section of the guide.

Test your knowledge

 Don't forget to go online for further self-tests on the text:
www.philipallan.co.uk/literatureguidesonline

Introduction

Approaching the text

A play is, above all, a narrative. A large part of the storyteller's art is to make you want to find out what happens next, and therefore to keep you reading to the end. In order to study *An Inspector Calls* and to enjoy it, you need to keep a close track of the events that take place in it. This guide will help you to do that, but you may also benefit from keeping your own notes on the main events and who is involved in them.

However, any play consists of much more than its events. You need to know the story well to get a good grade in the exam, but if you spend a lot of time simply retelling the story you will not get a high mark. You also need to keep track of a number of other features.

First, you need to take notice of the setting of the play — where the events take place — and how this influences the story. You also need to get to know the characters and how Priestley lets us know what they are like. Notice what they say and do, and what other people say about them. Think about why they behave in the way they do — their motives — and what clues the playwright gives us about these in terms of stage directions and comments by other characters. When you watch a production, also consider actors' facial expressions and body language, as they will give you clues about what the characters are thinking and feeling.

As you read on, you will notice themes: the ideas explored by the playwright. You may find it easier to think about these if you discuss them with other people. You should also try to become aware of the style of the play, especially on a second reading. This means how the playwright presents the story. The context, or background, of the play is also important.

All these aspects of the play are dealt with in this guide. However, you should always try to notice them for yourself. This guide is no substitute for a careful and thoughtful reading of the text.

Revising the text

An Inspector Calls may be one of your English Literature set texts for examination or it could be one of the texts you use in a Controlled Assessment. In either case, knowing the text is essential. Making sure that you read the play and keep good notes throughout your GCSE will help you; so too will proper revision and using this guide. In your assessment, you may be allowed to use your text but it will have to be unannotated, so revision is really important.

It is a good idea to get the date of your exam or Controlled Assessment well in advance so that you can plan a revision timetable in the lead-up to the assessment. Give yourself plenty of time, especially if you have other subjects to revise for. For example, you should start revising before Christmas for a summer exam.

When you revise it is a good idea for you to:
- sit at a table
- revise for 40-minute periods
- take ten-minute breaks
- reward yourself for hard work
- make note cards
- make lists
- plan responses
- make up mnemonics for key points
- create colourful posters
- learn while listening to classical music
- have a learning manager to test you
- colour-code your text into key areas

Grade booster

Make sure you know the play. To achieve a top grade, reread the play before your assessment.

Grade booster

Most importantly, use techniques that work for you.

Stage interpretations

Playwrights write plays in order for them to be performed — so as well as reading the play, it's a good idea for you to watch it, either as a film or at the theatre. This will help you write or speak more confidently about the text in an exam or Controlled Assessment. It will particularly help you if you are studying towards Edexcel's Controlled Assessment and wish to respond to the stagecraft task.

The 1954 black and white film of *An Inspector Calls* directed by Guy Hamilton is a screen adaptation of the play, well worth watching. It plays on the eerie nature of the Inspector's visit, with ominous sound effects, music and lighting. The film focuses viewers' attentions on particular characters, as their faults are exposed. Note characters' facial expressions, body language and tone of voice. These will give you clues about how they are feeling and what they are thinking. They can indicate their guilt or innocence.

Sybil Birling (Olga Lindo) and the Inspector (Alastair Sim) in the 1954 film version of *An Inspector Calls*.

Watergate Prods./The Kobal Collection

In this film adaptation, although the Inspector's name is changed by the screenwriter Desmond Davis from Goole to Poole, Alastair Sim creates an effective 'impression of massiveness, solidity and purposefulness' in keeping with Priestley's original intentions.

The BBC's 1982 TV production of the play was never produced on DVD or video but can be seen if you contact the BBC. It is a faithful rendition of the play, if a little wooden.

However, nothing can replace seeing the play on stage. Stephen Daldry's West End production of *An Inspector Calls* has been running since 1992, and presents an interesting interpretation of the play. It has become a regular fixture, enjoying two West End runs, six national tours and a visit to Australia.

First staged in 1992 at the National Theatre in London, Daldry's production moves closer to the vision that Daldry believes Priestley intended. Rather than using a realistic setting as had been done for many years, Daldry decided to transform *An Inspector Calls* into what one critic described as an 'urgent expressionistic nightmare'.

Taking a radical approach to the text, Daldry presents the action of the play in a 1912 house on stilts, sitting in a desolate, rainy wasteland of 1945. Here, the Inspector is shown to be a ghostly time traveller forcing the Birlings to come out of what Daldry describes as 'their safe Edwardian environment' into 'a metaphorical landscape'. The landscape appears to

The house collapses in Stephen Daldry's 2009 production.

Photostage

be that of war-torn Britain but it could be any wasteland that has been produced by man's irresponsibility to fellow man. The combination of time settings in this production helps create the effect that it is not only the Inspector but history itself that judges the Birlings.

The house is presented as a character responding to the Inspector's will and symbolically collapsing when the Birlings' lies are revealed. Its collapse can also be interpreted as representing key moments in history — the destruction of buildings during the Second World War, the collapse of capitalism and the collapse of class distinctions (the coming together of upper and lower classes as a result of the war).

Grade *booster*

Incorporating information about stage productions into your writing in a fluent and relevant way will help you get the best grades. Adding it on as an afterthought or writing about interpretations as if they were what Priestley originally wrote will not. For example, saying that a hat rather than a dress is what Sheila tries on in Milwards will lose you marks. This may be what she does in the film adaptation but it is not what she does in the original play.

Review your learning

(Answers on p. 84)

1 Besides the story of the play, what other aspects should you be aware of?

2 List three grade booster tips.

3 List a few helpful suggestions for revision.

4 In what way is Stephen Daldry's production of the play radical?

 More interactive questions and answers online.

Context

- What does the term 'context' mean?
- What does the context of the play tell us about its purpose?
- How does Priestley relate the events in the play to those in the wider world?
- How does Priestley show tensions between classes?

The context of a text refers to the circumstances at the time the text was written — in other words, what was happening in society, the literary world and historically when it was written. *An Inspector Calls* was written in 1945, the year in which the Second World War ended, but it is set in 1912, just before the First World War. Understanding the events which occurred in Britain and the world in the years leading up to and between these wars will help you to understand the context of the play. So too will knowing a bit about Priestley's own background.

J. B. Priestley in the 1970s.

Priestley's life

John Boynton Priestley was born on 13 September 1894 and grew up in the northern industrial town of Bradford (similar to the fictional Brumley of *An Inspector Calls*) during the late Victorian and early Edwardian eras. After leaving grammar school, Priestley worked in the wool trade despite having ambitions to become a writer. In his literary reminiscences, *Margin Released*, Priestley provides valuable insights into his working life, including a section on this period as a teenage clerk in a Bradford wool-sorter's office.

At the age of 18, Priestley volunteered for the army, serving in the 10th Batallion and fighting in France during the First World War. However, having been declared unfit for active duty following a gas attack, he went on to study at Cambridge

TopFoto

University where he completed a degree in Modern History and Political Science which informed his writing thereafter.

In 1921 he went to London to work as a freelance writer, fast gaining a reputation as a commentator on literature. He wrote a number of novels, his first, *The Good Companions*, being published in 1929, closely followed by his second, *Angel Pavement*, in 1930. In 1933 his role as a social commentator became apparent with his novel *English Journey*, which recorded what he saw and heard on his travels around England. His commentating continued with a series of articles and broadcasts.

At the age of 38, he wrote his first play, *Dangerous Corner*. This was followed by a string of plays, including *I Have Been Here Before* and *Time and the Conways*, both of which deal with the passage of time, as Priestley was influenced by J. W. Dunne's theories about time and the consequences of people's actions.

The playwright's interest in the problem of time led him, in 1964, to publish *Man and Time*, an extended essay. In this book he explored various theories and beliefs about time as well as his own research and conclusions.

Grade *booster*

Knowing about Priestley's background will help you to write more confidently about what influenced his writing of the play.

Key terms

Term	Definition
Conservatism	Political belief that seeks to preserve traditional values and whatever is seen as good in the country, and opposes radical change
Conservative	A member of the Conservative Party or anyone who has social or political views favouring conservatism
Right-wing	Term describing someone who supports political, social or economic conservatism, believing that things are better left unchanged
Socialism	An economic system based on collective ownership — usually state ownership of money and industry
Socialist	Someone who believes in socialism
Left-wing	Term describing someone who is not closely bound to traditional ways and is supportive of government intervention to cure social problems
Welfare state	A set of government programmes that aim to provide economic security for the population by providing for people when they are unemployed, ill or elderly
Labour Party	A left-wing political party
Liberalism	A political philosophy that favours social progress by reform and by changing laws rather than by revolution; an economic theory that promotes free competition and a self-regulating market
Liberal	Someone who has political or social views favouring reform and progress, free competition and a self-regulating market

Alongside this fascination with time, responsibility features as a theme in many of Priestley's plays, including *An Inspector Calls*, indicating Priestley's strong social conscience. Actively involved in politics, he chaired the 1941 Committee and co-founded the socialist Common Wealth Party.

During the Second World War, Priestley hosted a radio programme called *Postscripts* which gained a huge following, but was cancelled when the Conservative Party accused Priestley of expressing 'left-wing' views on the show. Despite this, Priestley continued to write and actively commentate on world affairs during this time and throughout his life. The political content of his broadcasts and his hopes for a new and different future influenced the politics of the postwar period and helped the Labour Party gain its landslide victory in 1945. He was at the forefront of the Campaign for Nuclear Disarmament (CND) and was a British delegate for UNESCO.

Priestley received several honours later in his life, including the Freedom of the City of Bradford and an honorary degree from Bradford University. In 1977, having previously declined both a knighthood and a

Suffragettes marching in London in 1910.

TopFoto

peerage, he was awarded the Order of Merit, a title he readily accepted as it was a gift from the sovereign, not linked to a political party.

Over the course of his life Priestley wrote more than 50 plays, most famous of which were *Dangerous Corner, When We Are Married* and *An Inspector Calls*. He died on 14 August 1984, aged 89.

In the lead-up to 1914

Priestley wrote *An Inspector Calls* following a time which had seen great activity both politically and in society. He set the play at a time when the need to improve working conditions for the poor was receiving considerable attention. In the five or six years before 1914, there had been mass unrest among the working classes in Britain. The number of people receiving charitable aid from the Church, or from associations like the fictional Brumley Women's Charity Organization in *An Inspector Calls*, had increased; of the 33 million people in the country, 10 million were living in destitution. In 1906 jobless people marched from the Midlands to London to protest at Downing Street, and in this same year, the Liberal Party gained a landslide victory against the Conservatives, signalling the unhappiness of the population and a change in people's attitudes.

In 1908, there was a cotton workers' strike and a suffragettes' demonstration, as votes for women became another hot topic politically. In response to Mr Birling's attempts to shield Sheila from events, the Inspector tells him that his daughter 'isn't living on the moon'. Priestley's audience at the time would have understood how relevant this statement was, given the changes in attitudes towards women.

In 1909, the new government introduced a 'People's Budget' — raising taxes in order to pay for social reform. The following year, there was a miners' strike and 700 mills in Lancashire locked out workers who were demanding higher wages. Priestley clearly drew on this when he created his characters of Mr Birling and Eva Smith. In 1912 nationwide riots occurred and 300,000 mill workers protested against low wages, once again being locked out by the owners. Low pay and rising prices meant that the working classes could barely survive. Eric's sympathetic attitude towards the working classes in the play shows that he is more liberal politically than his father. The fact that 2,500 children died in 1911 due to a heatwave and London was then seen as the second unhealthiest city in the world must have influenced Priestley's writing.

By 1912, when the play is set, 2% of Londoners were dying each week from the cold. This was also the year when plans to extend National Insurance to include medical aid for the poor were introduced, so

Mrs Birling's refusal to help Eva Smith is set against this backdrop. 1912 was also the year when the *Titanic* sank, despite Mr Birling's assertions that the ship is 'absolutely unsinkable'. Sick and maternity benefits first started in 1913, in the same year that 400 miners died in a pit fire and 500,000 British children were described by the Chief Medical Officer to Schools as being ill-fed and diseased.

Priestley was 18 when the First World War started in 1914. Mr Birling's assertion that talk of war was 'fiddlesticks' in a play set in 1912 for a postwar audience is clearly laughable. With its use of modern killing technology, the war proved to be a time of 'fire, blood and anguish', as the Inspector in the play warns. Income tax doubled in order to pay for the war, which cost £1 million a day. In 1914, 20,000 builders and 140,000 miners went on strike.

Between the wars

With men away at war and plans for compulsory conscription, women were urged to work in factories. Strikes continued in this period and women workers started to demand equal pay. By the end of the First World War, 10 million men had died. Priestley had suffered himself, having been exposed to a German gas attack and been declared unfit for active service. Rationing was introduced on petrol, gas, coal, electricity and meat, and the school leaving age was raised to 14.

In 1918 2,225 people in London died in a flu epidemic. Also in this year, the abolition of workhouses was proposed and women voted for the first time. Strikes continued and by 1921 unemployment figures had risen to 2.2 million. Throughout the 1920s, workers' unions continued to use strikes as a tool to demand higher wages in the face of rising costs of living. When Mr Birling talks of 'Capital versus Labour agitations' in the play he is referring to strikes.

In 1933, Hitler was elected Chancellor of Germany. The Fascist movement was gaining popularity in Britain, with anti-Jewish violence rising throughout Europe. The Great Depression began in 1929 with mass unemployment, highlighting the falseness in Mr Birling's 1912 belief in 'steadily increasing prosperity'. By 1939 the Second World War had started. In 1942 the welfare state was proposed, something of which Priestley, as a left-wing supporter, would have been in favour. In Daldry's production of the play 30 extras witness Eric's confession, representing the 1945 voters who ushered in the welfare state.

By 1945, the year Priestley wrote the play, the Second World War had ended with 55 million people dead, the Russian Revolution had occurred and the atom bomb had been dropped on Hiroshima. Priestley had seen all of this, so in setting his play in 1912, before either war had happened, and at a time of innocence and hope, he conveys his message of collective social responsibility even more powerfully.

Class system

At the time the play is set, Britain had just come out of a reign under King Edward VII, a larger-than-life man who enjoyed good food, sport and pretty women. The fashionable and highest classes of society followed his example and many in the upper classes enjoyed a life of leisure and socialising, ordered by the strictest rules of etiquette.

Even after Edward's death in 1910, the culture of the upper classes continued to be one of opulence and festivity. People tried desperately to outdo each other. Outside appearances were paramount. Husbands and wives could have affairs as long as family life was maintained. As long as the upper class's strict code of behaviour was followed and one had enough money to maintain appearances, then one was accepted in the Edwardian period.

However, this life of extravagance was reserved for the very richest. Most people in Britain were not part of this privileged minority. Although the Birlings are wealthy they are not presented as part of this high society, but as upper middle class. Mr Birling did not inherit his money; he worked hard for it. In 1912, the upper middle classes were more concerned with respectability than flamboyant displays of wealth. However, the conservatives in this class would have resented socialist ideas being put forward by writers such as 'these Bernard Shaws and H. G. Wellses', as Birling says, because, unlike those in the highest parts of society, they owned the factories that were being threatened by strikes at the time.

The lower classes in Britain were made up of people like Edna, the Birlings' maid, and Eva Smith, a factory worker. These people had often come from rural towns to big cities in search of work, only to find their working days long and their living conditions poor. Working-class workers earned about £1.12 a week (twenty-two and six) whereas someone like Mr Birling would have earned about £5.75 a week, although his salary would have been determined by the profits from his company.

By 1945, when Priestley wrote the play, he and others had seen two world wars greatly reduce distinctions between classes. In setting his play in 1912, at a time when class distinctions were clearer, Priestley created a powerful message of equality for his postwar audience.

Grade *focus*

You won't be assessed on context on its own, but you may get a question about how relevant the play is today and some boards assess context in their literature assessments (look at the *Assessment Objectives and skills* section for details of AO4). It is the sign of a high-level candidate to be able to incorporate relevant contextual information into an essay in a consistent and informed way. Writing one paragraph about context and then never mentioning it again will get you some marks but is the sign of someone working at the lower end of the grades. Use the table below to help you understand how, when writing about Mr Birling, you could incorporate context for different grades.

Grades A*–C	Grades D–G
Mr Birling fires Eva Smith as he is conservative in his approach. He views things from an industrialist and traditional point of view. Conservatism at the time represented the views of businesses (like Birling and Co. and Crofts Ltd) and landed people (like Gerald).	Mr Birling fires Eva Smith.
The play was written at a time when the welfare state was being introduced so Mr Birling's comments about responsibility would have been seen as very traditional.	Mr Birling is only concerned with self-interest. He does not believe in community.
Mr Birling has married up — his wife is his social superior. Movement between classes was difficult at the time the play is set and this explains why Mr Birling wants Sheila to marry Gerald, who comes from 'an old country family — landed people'.	Mr Birling is a self-made businessman and his wife is his social superior.
Mr Birling snaps at Eric as their political views are different. Eric is more liberal and Mr Birling feels threatened by reform, fearing loss of position in society, which is why he warns Eric that his ideas may lead him never to 'be in a position to let anybody to stay or anybody to go'. Eric represents the changing political attitudes and Mr Birling the traditional attitudes.	Mr Birling and his son do not get on. Eric sees things from Eva's perspective but Mr Birling doesn't.
Priestley was a socialist. He uses the contrast between the Inspector's socialist message and Mr Birling's conservative ideals to highlight the dangers in a lack of collective social responsibility.	The Inspector tries to get Mr Birling to see how important collective social responsibility is but Mr Birling will not take responsibility for the consequences of his actions.
Priestley uses dramatic irony to highlight the folly of Mr Birling's comments about society, war and the Titanic in his speeches to his children. A 1945 audience can clearly see how short-sighted Mr Birling is.	Mr Birling's speech about war and the *Titanic* is dramatically ironic as the audience knows that the *Titanic* sank and war happened.

Theatre at the time the play was written

During the First World War, theatre-goers had sought relief and pleasure from performances and this search for pleasure continued after 1918. Essentially, drama of the interwar years remained Edwardian in morality and theme. While the end of the First World War brought a temporary boom, it also brought a change in the way theatres were managed. This, along with the emergence of talking cinema in 1926 and the rise of an educated working class, meant that popular taste and its desire for novelty determined how successful a play was. Drawing-room comedies, classic revivals, escapist musicals and comic reviews were popular.

However, with the coming of the Second World War, its air raids and blackouts, theatres were forced to open and close erratically, so when Priestley completed *An Inspector Calls* in 1945, he sent it to Moscow. It was here that it was first performed, in 1945, by two companies simultaneously — Tairov's Kamerny Theatre and the Leningrad Comedy Theatre. It is significant that the play was first perfomed in Russia, a country that, after the Russian Revolution, had been founded on the ideals of equality for all. It wasn't until the following year that *An Inspector Calls* received its West End debut at the New Theatre in London.

Review your learning

(Answers on p. 84)

1 What does 'context' mean?

2 What parts of his life did Priestley draw on in *An Inspector Calls*?

3 What aspects of a 1912 setting are particularly relevant to the play?

4 How did Priestley draw on postwar events in his play?

 More interactive questions and answers online.

Plot and structure

- What are the main events of the play?
- How do the main storylines develop through the play?
- How is time represented in the play?

Act One

- The Birlings are celebrating Sheila's engagement to Gerald.
- Mr Birling is making speeches.
- The engagement ring is presented and the ladies and Eric depart.
- Mr Birling confides in Gerald about his knighthood and the two of them joke about the possibility of scandal.
- Eric returns and complains about the women's talk of clothes.
- Mr Birling states that a man has to look after himself and his family, no one else. He describes community as nonsense.
- The Inspector is at the front door.
- Mr Birling tries to influence the Inspector but he is unimpressed and explains his reason for calling at the house: a young girl has died in the infirmary.
- After being shown a photograph of the girl and recognising her, Mr Birling's part in Eva Smith's fate is revealed: he sacked her for asking for higher wages.
- Sheila returns and the Inspector continues his questioning. She is upset at Eva's dismissal.
- The Inspector suggests that it is not just Mr Birling who is involved and Mr Birling relaxes a little.
- Sheila is shown a photograph of the girl and rushes out of the room upset.
- Birling leaves to check on Sheila and tell his wife what is happening.
- When Sheila returns she confesses that she had the girl sacked from Milwards.
- Sheila is made to feel awful before the Inspector reveals that Eva changed her name to Daisy Renton.
- Gerald reacts sharply to this and the Inspector leaves to find Mr Birling.
- Sheila confronts Gerald, who admits to having had an affair with Daisy. Sheila warns him not to hide the truth.

The Birling family's home in the 2001 production at the Playhouse Theatre, London.

Priestley establishes the family setting and relative wealth of the household early in the play. The curtain rises to reveal a comfortable Edwardian family home, and at the start of the play we see the Birling family enjoying a celebratory dinner with Gerald Croft, son of a rival businessman to Mr Birling. We discover that Sheila has recently become engaged to Gerald and Mr Birling is in a good mood, as a result of the engagement and his upcoming knighthood. Mr Birling makes a number of speeches that express his views on the chances of war and the *Titanic* being unsinkable, and show him to be a short-sighted person.

Priestley makes first reference to the tensions between Eric and Mr Birling as Eric tells his father not to do any speech-making. There is also a hint that Eric may know something about Gerald's affair (which is later revealed) as he suddenly laughs inexplicably (H3). In the first moments of the play, Priestley gives us an insight into individual characters, their circumstances, wealth and relationships, as well as hinting at some key themes.

Using carefully timed exits and entrances, Priestley allows information about characters and events to be leaked to the audience in a particular order. Eric, Sheila and Mrs Birling exit the dining room leaving Gerald and Mr Birling to talk together. Mr Birling shows his concern for social

Pause for thought

What evidence can you find that Eric has been drinking? Is there any evidence that Mrs Birling knows and is uncomfortable about his drinking?

standing when he confides in Gerald about his knighthood, before Eric returns and the conversation once again turns to Mr Birling's views on life. He makes clear, to Gerald and Eric, his opinion on community, saying that a man should take care of only himself and his family, no one else. Priestley hence establishes collective responsibility as a key theme in the play. Little does Mr Birling know that his views on community are about to be put to scrutiny.

Mr Birling's expression of his narrow view of responsibility is the cue for the doorbell which signals the Inspector's arrival and interupts the evening. Mr Birling and Gerald make a joke about Eric having been up to mischief and Eric takes offence at this, revealing his relative isolation from his father and possible guilty conscience. Edna, the parlour maid, announces the entrance of Inspector Goole. Mr Birling wrongly assumes that the Inspector may have called about a warrant but we soon discover that he is making enquiries into the suicide of a young woman called Eva Smith, who has died in the infirmary after drinking some disinfectant.

Mr Birling's arrogance is ruffled when the Inspector shows him a photograph of the woman and Mr Birling recognises her. Priestley sets up events so that only Mr Birling sees the photograph. This will prove useful later when Gerald argues that the Inspector does not exist.

Mr Birling admits that he once employed Eva Smith in his factory and, as a result of the Inspector's questions, he goes on to reveal that he had her sacked because of an industrial dispute over wages. Priestley reveals the tensions between Mr Birling and Eric, which become more apparent when Eric shows a more liberal attitude to the situation, only for his father to shout him down and embarrass him.

Priestley uses characters to explore political or moral stances. The differing attitudes of characters are shown by Sheila's remonstrations that 'these girls aren't cheap labour' but 'people', and Mr Birling's and Gerald's belief that Mr Birling acted within reason. Eric and Sheila feel that their father was callous in sacking the girl. Priestley contrasts Sheila's show of compassion here with her revelations later. When Sheila is shown a photograph of the girl, with Priestley again controlling the situation so that she sees it on her own, she recognises the girl, becomes upset and runs out of the room. Mr Birling exits to see what is wrong with Sheila and also to tell his wife what is happening.

By including this exit, Priestley allows Gerald and Eric to speak to the Inspector on their own. Gerald asks to see the photograph that Sheila has seen but is prevented from doing so as the Inspector says 'all in good time'. Priestley is therefore able to establish through the Inspector the idea of a chain of events and the Inspector's desire to follow one line of enquiry at a time. Gerald's objections foreshadow his later suspicions about the Inspector and the photograph. His comment about 'respectable citizens' also identifies a key theme — the difference between law and morality. Eric's exchange with the Inspector reveals that he is a drinker and indicates that the Inspector intends to question Eric also. Priestley therefore establishes that both Gerald and Eric have played a part in the girl's fate.

Sheila re-enters and it is then that her part in Eva Smith's life is revealed. She admits to having had the woman sacked from her job as a shop assistant at Milwards because a dress had suited her better than Sheila and she had smiled when Sheila tried it on. Sheila shows some regret for her actions.

The Inspector announces that Eva Smith had used more than one name, and had in fact changed her name to Daisy Renton. The reaction that this revelation causes in Gerald makes it obvious that he knows her. The Inspector enquires after Mr Birling, and Sheila asks Eric to show him to the drawing room where Mr Birling is. Priestley once again uses an exit in order to allow characters to talk in private. This gives Sheila time to talk to Gerald about his reaction. He admits to having had an affair with the girl but asks Sheila to keep it from the Inspector. She realises that this is foolish, recognising the omniscience of the Inspector: 'I hate to think how much he knows that we don't know yet.' She ends by warning Gerald, 'You'll see. You'll see,' and just at that moment Priestley heightens the tension by having the Inspector enter, concluding the act with the ominous question 'Well?' and at a moment of suspense.

> ### Pause for thought
>
> Although Sheila shows regret for her actions, we are left initially in some doubt as to whether this is because she had an impact on the girl's life or because she can never feel comfortable at Milwards again. Look carefully at what Sheila says and find evidence to show this is the case.

Act Two

- Sheila remains in the dining room despite Gerald's objections.
- Mrs Birling returns and tries to intimidate the Inspector by reminding him of her husband's social standing.
- Sheila warns her not to build up a wall as this will only be knocked down by the Inspector.
- Eric's drinking is revealed and Mrs Birling is shocked.
- Gerald initially tries to deny his link with Daisy but then reveals details of their affair.
- He says he met her in the Palace Bar and discovered she had no food and no home, so installed her in a friend's rooms.
- Sheila notices that Gerald was not shown a photograph of the girl.
- Mrs Birling is shown a photograph of the girl and claims not to know her.

1

- The Inspector accuses her of lying and Mrs Birling demands an apology.
- The Inspector refuses and Sheila tells her mother to tell the truth.
- The front door slams and Mr Birling returns to say Eric has left. The Inspector hints that Eric is needed.
- Mrs Birling admits her involvement with the girl — she had denied her help when she came to Brumley Women's Charity Organization two weeks previously.
- Mrs Birling says that she did nothing wrong and that the man who got Eva Smith pregnant should be held responsible.
- Sheila warns her mother to stop talking as she (and the audience) can see that the man Mrs Birling is referring to is in fact Eric.
- Eric returns to the dining room.

The Inspector's entrance allows him to question Gerald. At first, Gerald says that he wants Sheila to leave so that she is shielded from anything 'unpleasant and disturbing', but Sheila insists on staying.

By now there is evident tension between Sheila and Gerald, which Priestley highlights through the characters' emotive statements and the stage directions which indicate a bitter tone. Priestley then uses the Inspector as a narrative device to explain Sheila's motivations for wishing to stay to hear Gerald's story.

Gerald Croft (Timothy Watson, left) and Inspector Goole (Nicholas Woodeson) in Stephen Daldry's 2009 production.

Mrs Birling's entrance (H29) facilitates a number of developments: we gain an insight into her pompous character and are shown her attitude towards class and social standing. She reminds the Inspector of her husband's position in society and talks dismissively of 'girls of that class' in an attempt to influence others' perceptions and distance herself from events. We are also shown the difference between her and Sheila in their attitudes towards the Inspector and responsibility. It is during this time, with Mr Birling and Eric absent, that Priestley allows Eric's drinking to be revealed.

Mr Birling re-enters, telling the others that he has been trying to persuade Eric to go to bed, but that he has refused because he knows the Inspector wishes to question him. We are reminded of Priestley's well-made play (see page 53) through the Inspector's reference to his organised line of enquiry, as he makes clear to Mr Birling that Eric will have to 'wait his turn' to be questioned, despite Mr Birling's suggestion that he question him now. Sheila appears to recognise the significance of this, and the impression the Inspector has made on her becomes evident in her comments and her 'over-excited' behaviour. Unlike the others she can see the omniscience of the Inspector.

This becomes heightened when Gerald attempts to lie and Sheila tells him 'It's no use, Gerald. You're wasting time.' After a bitter remark from Sheila and further questions from the Inspector, Gerald finally admits that he had an affair with Daisy Renton in the spring of the previous year. He says that they met at the Palace music hall in Brumley and that she had been 'wedged' into a corner by 'Joe Meggarty'. Gerald tells how he helped Daisy and after two nights discovered that she had no money or home, so 'installed' her in some rooms belonging to a friend who was abroad.

The Inspector asks Gerald if he was in love with Daisy and Mr Birling protests but is quickly put in his place by the Inspector: 'Why should you do any protesting? It was you who turned the girl out in the first place.' Priestley once again uses the Inspector as a choric device, reminding the audience of Mr Birling's part in Eva's life. When Mr Birling explains that he doesn't want Sheila to be 'dragged into this', Priestley highlights changing attitudes to women through the Inspector, who points out to Mr Birling that his daughter is 'not living on the moon', and Sheila insists on staying to hear what Gerald has to say.

Gerald explains that he broke things off with Daisy at the end of the summer, and Priestley cleverly uses the device of a diary to fill in events as the Inspector reveals that Daisy had kept a diary which told of how happy she had been and how she wanted to go away for a while 'just to

Pause for thought

Priestley structures his play carefully. Consider how Gerald's exit is used. What does it allow him to do that later proves to be useful?

Pause for thought

Why do you think Priestley has the Inspector question Mrs Birling before Eric even though her involvement with Eva Smith occurred after Eric's? How does this choice contribute to the play?

Key quotation

'I didn't see any reason to believe that one story should be any truer than the other. Therefore, you're quite wrong to suppose that I shall regret what I did.'

(Mrs Birling, H47, L15–18)

make it last longer'. Gerald, appearing upset, asks to leave for a walk but before he goes Sheila returns her engagement ring to him.

While feeling angry with Gerald for his involvement with the girl, Sheila admits to having a certain respect for him once he has told the truth. However, she stands by her decision despite her father's remonstrations, telling him not to interfere.

Thinking the issue has been resolved, Mrs Birling is shown a photograph of the girl. She says she doesn't recognise her. However, the Inspector accuses her of lying. Mrs Birling is shocked at the Inspector's rudeness but he refuses to apologise for doing his duty and Mr Birling once again highlights that he is a 'public man'. The Inspector's response makes clear his — and Priestley's — view that public men have responsibilities as well as privileges. Mr Birling tries to intimidate the Inspector and control the situation. In contrast, Sheila feels that it is foolish to try and hinder the Inspector's enquiries and this appears to be well founded. The difference between how Mr and Mrs Birling and Sheila view responsibilities becomes clear before a door is heard shutting and Mr Birling exits to investigate.

Pause for thought

Do you think Sheila is right to reject Gerald? Look at what she says here and later in the play. Are there any indications that she may change her mind later?

Priestley deliberately orchestrates events so that only Mrs Birling and Sheila are left in the dining room. This allows the Inspector to begin his questioning of Mrs Birling, without any men — and significantly, without Eric — present.

At the point when Eric is out of the room Mrs Birling is forced to admit that she also had an involvement with the girl. We are told that two weeks earlier she had used her position as a prominent member of the Brumley Women's Charity Organization to refuse the girl help when she appealed to them. She gives as a reason the fact that Eva Smith had at first lied to her about her name, calling herself Mrs Birling. It is then revealed that the girl was pregnant and that Mrs Birling did not believe her story about refusing money from the father of her unborn child. Mrs Birling insists that she has done nothing wrong.

Priestley builds tension and uses proleptic (anticipated) irony (see p. 57) when he presents Mrs Birling as being tricked by the Inspector into stating that the father of the unborn child was 'entirely responsible' and ought to be 'compelled to confess in public his responsibility'. The audience and Sheila are aware of how the finger of suspicion now points at Eric as being the father of the unborn child, but it is only when the Inspector says that he is waiting to do his duty, as Mrs Birling has advised him to do, that Mrs Birling finally realises that her son is implicated. At this crucial moment, Priestley uses the device of a door slamming — the front door — to heighten suspense as the characters and the audience look expectantly towards the door, expecting Eric, who then enters. Once again Priestley creates suspense, and ends the act on a cliffhanger.

Act Three

- Eric realises that they all know he had some involvement with Eva Smith.
- Eric admits that he met Eva at the Palace Bar and forced himself on her.
- Mrs Birling is shocked and upset, so Sheila takes her out of the room.
- Eric continues his story, revealing how he had made Eva pregnant and, after offering to marry her, stolen money from his father to help her.
- Sheila and Mrs Birling return and Mr Birling fills his wife in on developments.
- Mr Birling starts to think of how he can cover things up.
- Eric finds out that his mother denied Eva help. He accuses Mrs Birling of killing her own grandchild.
- The Inspector reminds them of their actions and warns them that if people do not choose to learn lessons then they will be forced to — in fire, blood and anguish. He then leaves.
- The family argue about events and Mr Birling worries about his knighthood.
- Sheila starts to wonder about the Inspector's arrival and whether he was a real policeman.
- The others think they can avoid scandal if he is found not to be a real policeman.
- Gerald returns and Sheila is kept from telling him about the confessions of Eric and Mrs Birling.
- Gerald says that Inspector Goole does not exist and Mr Birling confirms this by phoning his friend the Chief Constable.
- Gerald calls the infirmary and discovers there have been no suicides for months.
- The elder Birlings and Gerald seem relieved at this but Eric and Sheila think it makes no difference.
- Gerald offers Sheila her engagement ring back.
- The phone rings — it is the police telling them that there has been a suicide at the infirmary and an inspector is calling round to ask some questions.

Pause for thought

Priestley allows Eric to reveal his part in Eva Smith's life last. Why do you think this is?

Eric enters and immediately senses that everyone knows the truth. Priestley presents relationships between family members as starting to break down; Sheila tells Eric that Mrs Birling has been blaming him and then admits to having told Mrs Birling about his drinking. Eric is angry at both women, and Mr Birling reminds Sheila of family loyalty before the Inspector continues his enquiries into the girl's suicide, advising Mr Birling that 'There'll be plenty of time, when I've gone, for you all to adjust your family relationships.'

Eric explains how he met Eva Smith in the Palace Bar, how he had been drinking and was 'a bit squiffy' and insisted on taking her home. According to him 'that's when it happened'. The traditional Mrs Birling is shocked at this revelation and Mr Birling asks Sheila to take her out of the room. It is significant that the ladies should exit at this stage as Priestley is presenting a play set in 1912 with Mrs Birling demonstrating fairly traditional attitudes towards gender; she and her husband see it as inappropriate for her to remain to hear full details of Eric's involvement with Eva. Sheila's attitude towards gender is less traditional than her mother's and she wishes to remain, hence her 'protesting' comment, 'But — I want to — ,' in response to her father's instruction to take her mother out of the room.

Pause for thought

How are men and women presented in the play? Look at the way Mrs Birling and Sheila behave and talk. Look also at references to women throughout the play. What evidence is there of different characters' attitudes towards gender in the play?

Pause for thought

What is your view of Eric and his behaviour? Who do you think has acted in a worse manner, Eric or Gerald? Find evidence to support your ideas.

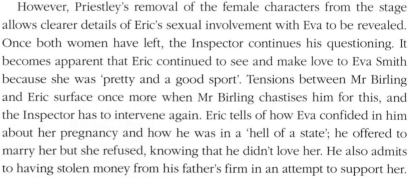

However, Priestley's removal of the female characters from the stage allows clearer details of Eric's sexual involvement with Eva to be revealed. Once both women have left, the Inspector continues his questioning. It becomes apparent that Eric continued to see and make love to Eva Smith because she was 'pretty and a good sport'. Tensions between Mr Birling and Eric surface once more when Mr Birling chastises him for this, and the Inspector has to intervene again. Eric tells of how Eva confided in him about her pregnancy and how he was in a 'hell of a state'; he offered to marry her but she refused, knowing that he didn't love her. He also admits to having stolen money from his father's firm in an attempt to support her.

Mrs Birling and Sheila return and are told about developments. Mr Birling is angry with Eric for not coming to him despite Eric's explanation that he is 'not the kind of father a chap could go to when he's in trouble'. The entrance of the two women allows Sheila and the Inspector to reveal to Eric Mrs Birling's involvement with Eva. When he hears that Mrs Birling refused to help the girl, he is horrified and blames her for the death of both the girl and the unborn child.

It is clear that family unity has entirely dissolved. At this key moment, Priestley has the Inspector, who recognises that his job is done, make a speech about the consequences of every character's actions and their combined responsibility for the chain of events that led to Eva Smith's suicide. He shows how each character has played a part in ruining the girl's life and states that he does not think any of them will forget what they have done.

Priestley uses the Inspector as a vehicle to remind the characters and audience that we are all collectively responsible for our actions, because they have consequences and affect other people's lives. He warns the characters of the dangers of not recognising that 'We are members of one body' who are 'responsible for each other'. This is in direct contrast with the speeches made by Mr Birling at the start of the play. Prophetically the Inspector warns us of the need to learn 'that lesson'. He says that if the lesson of collective social responsibility is not readily learned, then men will be 'taught it in fire and blood and anguish', before he finally leaves.

The mood changes once the Inspector has gone as characters are left to consider their actions. Priestley shows how each character reacts to events. Mr Birling blames Eric for his behaviour. He is concerned about possible scandal and how this will affect his chances of a knighthood. Eric says he is ashamed of his parents but Mr Birling insists that they have done nothing wrong and were justified in their actions. Sheila recognises that her parents don't appear to have learnt anything and Priestley uses Eric to reinforce this message when he talks of Mr Birling's foolish speech about community and the timing of the Inspector's entrance. Sheila is struck by

Text **focus**

'But don't you see…He was our police inspector all right.' (H59, L8–18)
At this crucial moment in the play when the Inspector has left and the elder Birlings attempt to distance themselves from their consciences and responsibilities, Priestley has Sheila remind us of what the Inspector called the 'chain of events'. She acts as the Inspector's voice in his absence, reminding us of what each of them did and the need for social conscience. Priestley uses Sheila and Eric as symbols of the changing social attitudes between the wars. Following Sheila's speech, Priestley makes clear that Eric too recognises that the Inspector's identity is immaterial. What matters is that he was 'our police inspector all right' — the characters' police inspector, regulating their behaviour and reminding them of the need for accountability.

this and begins to wonder whether he really was a police inspector. While recognising that this doesn't much matter now, she is the first to voice the question about the Inspector's identity. Her parents latch on to this, using it as an excuse to forget their actions. Sheila and Eric, however, are unable to do the same.

Sheila is the first to recognise the omniscience of the Inspector in Act One, and here again Priestley uses her as a vehicle to suggest that 'He never seemed like an ordinary police inspector', hinting at his prophetic and omniscient status. However, Sheila's comment also sets off Mr Birling's doubts about the Inspector's identity. He asserts that they have been 'bluffed' into confessing their actions and he returns to his earlier beliefs about liberals and humanitarians, calling the Inspector 'a Socialist or some sort of crank'.

When Gerald returns from his walk Sheila is stopped from telling him the details of Mrs Birling's and Eric's involvement with Eva Smith. He tells the others that the Inspector was not a police inspector (and explains that he had asked a police sergeant whether he knew of an Inspector Goole and he didn't). Mr Birling confirms this when he calls his friend Chief Constable Colonel Roberts. Gradually Gerald starts to prove that the Inspector was a hoax. He uses the uncertainty over the girl's name and the fact that not all of them necessarily saw the same photograph to prove that each of them could have interacted with a different girl.

Pause for thought

Gerald questions the truth and reality of the Inspector. What evidence is there in the play to suggest that Priestley wants us to question the nature of what we see?

This leads Gerald to question whether any girl has in fact died. When he calls the infirmary to check this, he discovers that no girl has died and that they haven't had a suicide for months.

Priestley now highlights the differences between characters in their attitudes to events. Mr Birling conveniently uses the fact that there was no suicide as 'proof positive' that the whole story is 'just a lot of moonshine', and he and his wife are happy to forget their actions and return to celebrations. However, Sheila and Eric are unable to forget and pretend 'everything's just as it was before'. They feel guilty about their actions and, unlike their parents and Gerald, they have been changed by the recent events. The others, however, feel a great sense of relief, their confidence in the rightness of their own actions having been restored.

Priestley ends the play with a surprising twist, for just as ease has been restored to Mr and Mrs Birling and Gerald, and they are ready to return to their comfortable and ignorant lives, the telephone rings and Mr Birling answers it. It is the police calling to advise the family that a girl has just died in the infirmary after swallowing some disinfectant and that a police inspector is on his way to ask some questions. Just as Mr Birling's narrow view of responsibility was the cue for the doorbell signalling the Inspector's entrance in Act One, here these three characters' refusal of responsibility is the cue for a telephone call signalling a return to the Inspector's message of responsibility. Despite — or perhaps because of — some of the characters' beliefs that they can avoid taking responsibility, Priestley reminds us that until we learn our lesson we will be taught it in 'fire and blood and anguish'.

Pause for thought

Do you think the police inspector at the end of the play will be the same one as at the start? Who do you think the Inspector is? What could he symbolise?

The timescale of the play

As in most **well-made plays** (see page 53), the majority of the action occurs before the actual play. The action on stage happens in real time and takes place over one evening. The following timeline gives you an idea of dates for the action both off and on stage.

Timeline

Time	What happens
September 1910	Eva Smith is sacked from Birling and Co.
December 1910	Eva is employed by Milwards
Late January 1911	Eva is sacked by Milwards
March 1911	Eva becomes involved with Gerald
Early September 1911	Gerald breaks off the affair Eva leaves Brumley for two months
November 1911	Eric meets Eva
December 1911/January 1912	Eva discovers that she is pregnant
Late March 1912	Mrs Birling refuses to help Eva
Early April 1912	The Birlings are celebrating their daughter's engagement and an Inspector calls, investigating Eva's suicide

The movement of tension as time progresses on stage

The following graph shows the increases and decreases in tension as time progresses on stage.

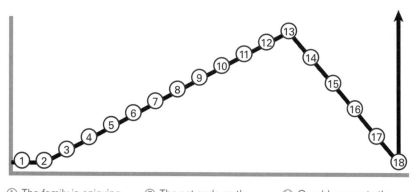

Grade *booster*

You are likely to be assessed on how the structure of the plot works. Showing how different parts of the plot contribute to the development of tension and suspense will help you to gain a higher grade than simply retelling the plot. For example, you could explain that the Inspector's exit in Act One allows Gerald and Sheila to talk in private about his affair before it is revealed publicly, rather than just saying that he leaves.

① The family is enjoying a celebration but there are hints of what is to come: 'except for all last summer when you never came near me'; 'she's got a nasty temper sometimes'.
② The doorbell sounds just as Mr Birling talks about his views on community.
③ The inspector enters.
④ Interrogation of Mr Birling.
⑤ Interrogation of Sheila.
⑥ Sheila questions Gerald.

⑦ The act ends as the Inspector re-enters, saying 'Well?'
⑧ Interrogation of Gerald.
⑨ Interrogation of Mrs Birling and her insistence that the Inspector should do his duty.
⑩ The act ends with Eric entering to a knowing crowd.
⑪ Eric's interrogation.
⑫ Inspector gives his final speech.
⑬ Inspector leaves.

⑭ Gerald suggests the inspector is not a policeman.
⑮ Gerald puts forward the idea that they weren't involved with the same girl.
⑯ There was no suicide at the infirmary.
⑰ Everything returns to how it was at the start.
⑱ A phone call from the police ends the play.

Review your learning

(Answers on p. 84)

❶ In Act One, what attitudes are shown by Birling, Eric and Gerald towards the sacking of Eva Smith?

❷ Whose confession follows Sheila's?

❸ How was Mrs Birling involved with Eva Smith?

❹ What information does Gerald bring when he returns from his walk in Act Three and why is this important?

More interactive questions and answers online.

Characterisation

- How does Priestley reveal the characters to us?
- What evidence is there to help us think about each character?
- What is each character like?
- What role does each character play?
- What are the relationships between characters?

Characters in a play are revealed to us through a combination of techniques:

- stage directions
- what characters say and do
- how they speak
- what others say and think about them
- what they think themselves

Mr Birling

- is a self-made businessman
- is smug
- is heavy-looking
- likes to lecture his children
- is more concerned with appearances than truth
- is a traditionalist
- is a social climber
- is socially inferior to his wife

Mr Birling is the first and last character in the play to speak, indicating his importance. He is described in stage directions as 'heavy-looking' and 'portentous', which suggests his opulent lifestyle and prophetic words. He is ex-lord mayor of Brumley, a local magistrate and up for a knighthood. His social standing is important to him and he tries to use his place in society to influence others and evade the law, warning the Inspector that he is an old friend of Chief Constable Colonel Roberts and threatening to report him.

Although provincial himself, Birling has married well; his wife is described as his 'social superior' and Birling shows that he recognises his social inadequacies when he confides in Gerald about his possible

> **Key quotation**
>
> 'I was an alderman for years — and Lord Mayor two years ago — and I'm still on the Bench.'
>
> (Mr Birling, H11, L19–21)

knighthood. Mr Birling is used by Priestley as an example of the rising upper middle classes in the Edwardian era.

Mr Birling has done well for himself by becoming a successful factory owner, and he recognises that his daughter's engagement to Gerald makes good business sense. While he says it is 'one of the happiest nights of his life', we discover that this is because he views the engagement as a business transaction which will enable a time when 'Crofts and Birlings are no longer competing but are working together — for lower costs and higher prices'. Mr Birling is a strong businessman — a self-confessed 'hard-headed practical man of business' who puts money and image above everything else, including his relationship with his son.

It is evident that Birling likes to think of himself as a family man. He makes reference to Sheila's engagement as a nice family celebration on a number of occasions and he says that a man has to look after not only himself but also 'his own', so he appears to have a strong regard for his family. However, when blame shifts from him to other members of his family in the Inspector's investigations, he is relieved, speaking 'with marked change of tone' and saying that 'this makes all the difference'. This suggests that he has no regard for individual family members but is more concerned with his family's social standing. He is protective of his daughter and tries to shield her from the Inspector's enquiries, offering to 'settle it sensibly' for her with the Inspector. Mr Birling holds traditional views regarding women and the younger generation so this may explain his behaviour here, but we may also presume that his reasons for wanting to shield Sheila relate to his concerns over public scandal.

Mr Birling's relationship with Eric is fraught. It is obvious that the two of them are not close. Mr Birling seems to favour Gerald, describing him as 'just the kind of son-in-law' he always wanted and sharing confidences and a joke with him. Although Mrs Birling is from a higher class, and assertive in her own right, Mr Birling is the head of the household; it is to his judgement that she tells the family to turn after the Inspector leaves, and it is he who tries to exert authority over Eric by shouting at and attacking him, and threatening to throw him out.

Mr Birling prides himself on his business sense, but is insensitive to the lives of others. Priestley uses him as a symbol of the callousness and heartlessness of capitalism. He openly states that he does not believe in 'community and all that nonsense', describing those who do as socialists and cranks. Viewing it as his duty to 'keep labour costs down', he shows no remorse for firing Eva Smith, and when he learns about Eric's involvement with her, his primary concern is with concealing the thefts. He is more worried about 'public scandal' than helping his son. He deludes himself into believing that just because the whole story 'was a lot of moonshine' his actions are unimportant, stating that, 'It makes all the difference.'

Smugly, Birling asserts that he would have spotted that the Inspector was a hoax if he hadn't arrived during their family celebration, and he and his wife unite in turning a blind eye to their misdemeanours. He fails to learn his lesson and take responsibility for his actions, until the very end when the telephone rings. Priestley describes Birling as 'panic-stricken' here, indicating that his defiance and bravado have finally been shattered.

Mrs Birling

- is Mr Birling's social superior
- is cold and unsympathetic
- is self-assured
- is prejudiced
- is hypocritical
- is selfish

> **Pause for thought**
>
> Do you think this actress has conveyed Mrs Birling's character well in this image?

Mrs Birling is first described in stage directions as 'about fifty, a rather cold woman and her husband's social superior', so immediately we gain the sense that she is an unfeeling individual who has enjoyed a privileged life. Like her husband, she is arrogant and tries to use her family's position in society to shirk her responsibilities, saying, 'You know of course that my husband was Lord Mayor only two years ago and that he's still a magistrate.'

Sybil Birling (Judy Parfitt) in Stephen Daldry's 1993 production.

When she first speaks we see that she is someone concerned with social etiquette. She admonishes her husband for his compliment to the cook, which she sees as inappropriate, and also for talking too much. She reprimands her daughter for contradicting her and on several occasions tells her to be quiet. She adheres to traditional gender roles, advising her daughter to get used to Gerald spending time and energy on his business and deferring to Gerald's judgement of Eric's drinking by saying 'and you're a man'.

When she enters the scene after the interrogation of Sheila and Mr Birling, she assumes a position of social superiority and confidence that Sheila recognises as misplaced. She refers to 'this absurd business', showing disgust at the situation and a lack of compassion for Eva Smith. She is very brisk and dismissive in her manner, calling Eva Smith 'the girl' in a prejudiced way, insinuating that her social position distances her from the Birlings: 'Girls of that class—' (H30). Mrs Birling is a snob who lacks compassion for others and refuses to acknowledge the suffering of those in the world outside her cosy home. While Sheila can see that there is no point in trying to 'build up a kind of wall' between herself and Eva Smith because the Inspector will simply 'break it down', Mrs Birling refuses to accept responsibility for her actions.

She shows an ignorance of the world around her, appearing shocked when Gerald refers to 'women of the town', and she is described as 'staggered' when she hears of Alderman Meggarty's behaviour. Her ignorance extends to her own family as she appears to be unaware of her son's drinking until the Inspector's visit. Mrs Birling is distanced from the world around her. She thinks that because Eva Smith is of a lower class she has no scruples or morals.

Text focus

'If you think you can bring any pressure to bear… change my mind.' (H44, L21–32)

Priestley shows here how unfeeling Mrs Birling is and how unwilling she is to accept responsibility for the consequences of her actions. She is insistent that she has done nothing shameful. In fact she asserts that she has done her 'duty', in an attempt to maintain an appearance of respectability. By referring to Eva Smith as 'the girl' Mrs Birling distances herself from her; and by saying that 'she seemed not to be a good case — and so I used my influence to have it refused', Mrs Birling shows that she has used her power to deny a needy individual help. Priestley presents Mrs Birling as an example of those in the middle class at the time who had no understanding of or compassion for others, and who misused their position in society. The number of times Mrs Birling repeats the word 'I' suggests her self-importance. It is both ironic and an indication of her hypocrisy that she says she is unwilling to permit the Inspector to use his power over her, when she has used her own power over Eva Smith. She clearly sees herself as being above the law.

Mrs Birling selfishly enjoys her position of power as a prominent member of the Brumley Women's Charity Organization and uses this to refuse Eva Smith help when she appeals to them. When the Inspector first asks Mrs Birling about this, her hesitation suggests her desire not to admit the truth, but when he continues with his questioning, she confidently and unfeelingly asserts that she has done nothing wrong.

When she is finally exposed, Mrs Birling remains adamant that what she has done is right: 'In the circumstances I think I was justified.' While she condemns Eva Smith for lying ('The girl had begun by telling us a pack of lies'), she is guilty of this herself. Mrs Birling is hypocritical, initially insisting that the man who made Eva Smith pregnant 'ought to be dealt with very severely', then refusing to take reponsibility for her words when this man is revealed to be Eric, her son: 'But I didn't know it was *you*.'

She praises Gerald and is 'grateful' to him for the way in which he argues his case 'cleverly', showing the Inspector to be a hoax, and she is happy to go on behaving in the same way as before. She, like her husband, thinks the whole thing is 'amusing', until she is forced to reassess the situation when she is told that an inspector is on his way to ask some questions. Priestley indicates that 'they stare dumbfounded', but in Daldry's West End production the two elder Birlings return to the restored house, signifying their refusal to change and their return to their previous beliefs and lives.

Sheila Birling (Marianne Oldham) in Stephen Daldry's 2009 production.

Sheila Birling

- is pretty
- is lively
- is self-centred
- is bad-tempered
- is remorseful
- takes responsibility for the consequences of her actions
- is used by Priestley to remind the audience of the 'chain of events' and the characters' roles in Eva's fate

Sheila is the daughter of the Birlings and at the start of the play the family is celebrating her promising engagement to Gerald Croft. Priestley describes Sheila as 'a pretty girl in her early twenties, very pleased with life and rather excited', so at the start of the play we see Sheila as an over-indulged young

Rex Features

girl, who enjoys a comfortable life. Her bad temper, which results in Eva Smith's dismissal, is hinted at by Priestley through Eric, early in the play, when he says 'she's got a nasty temper sometimes'.

However, through the course of the play we discover that Sheila is one of only two characters who appear to learn from their errors. She, like her brother Eric, is part of the 'younger generation'. This is significant, as Priestley through the Inspector suggests that the 'younger ones' are 'more impressionable', able to change — and therefore they offer us hope for a different and better future. Sheila is deeply affected by the Inspector's revelations. She takes responsibility for her actions, and expresses remorse: 'I'll never, never do it again to anybody.'

At times, she acts almost as an assistant to the Inspector, in that she supports his criticism of the other characters, even when he leaves the stage. Her parents take exception to her behaviour, seeing it as showing a lack of loyalty, and accuse her of being 'childish'. However, Sheila sees no point in concealing things. She, along with the Inspector, tries to get at the truth. She lacks the coldness of her parents and recognises that honesty and truth have a value that surpasses appearances; she says, 'it's you two who are being childish, trying not to face the facts.'

At a time of great social change with the introduction of the welfare state, Priestley uses Sheila as an example of people's changing attitudes towards those less fortunate than themselves. She is able to identify with the dead girl, because they were both pretty, about the same age, lively and outgoing. She is sympathetic towards her, recognising that such girls are not 'cheap labour', as her father believes, but 'people'.

However, while she feels sorry about the girl's dismissal from her father's factory, we can't help but recognise that Sheila's grievance against the girl when she worked at Milwards was malicious, and probably one of the least justified actions in the play. Sheila had the girl sacked just for smiling in what she thought was a critical way. It is clear that she was simply jealous of Eva Smith's attractiveness. Her actions were based entirely on self-centredness and vanity. However, during the course of the play Sheila matures. She shows that she feels bad about her actions and regrets them deeply, admitting honestly to her share of responsibility for the girl's fate.

Sheila symbolises the changing attitudes to women; she objects to her parents' and Gerald's attempts to stop her from speaking out, and to 'protect' her from the unpleasant truth: 'I'm not a child, don't forget. I've a right to know.'

Pause for thought

Do you think Sheila was to blame for her behaviour here or can you see any way of suggesting that Eva herself was to blame?

Sheila's sensitivity and alertness allow her to quickly realise what the Inspector is driving at in his interviews with people. She recognises how futile it is for the characters to cover up and lie about their actions. She can see in advance how unsuccessful her mother's confident manner and Gerald's attempt to conceal his affair will prove.

> **Key quotation**
>
> 'You'll see. You'll see.'
>
> (Sheila, H26, L29)

> **Key quotation**
>
> 'But, Mother, do stop before it's too late.'
>
> (Sheila, H31, L6)

Grade *booster*

Sheila is the first to recognise that the Inspector knows all about them — 'I hate to think how much he knows that we don't know yet' — and she is the first to know who the father of the baby is. Similarly, it is Sheila who first begins to wonder who the Inspector really is, both during his interrogations and after he has left. She is also the first to speak out about the way the family tries to pretend that nothing has happened, at the end of the play: 'You're pretending everything's just as it was before' (H71, L12–13). Use your knowledge of this to show that you can draw links between events and cross-refer. It will also show that you are aware of Sheila's role as an assistant to the Inspector and to Priestley as a playwright. These are higher-level skills than those involved in just writing about what Sheila does.

Sheila is frightened by the attitudes of her parents and Gerald, recognising that, although for a while it seemed as though they were learning something, their learning has stopped once they have seen a way out for themselves.

Sheila, and to a lesser extent her brother Eric, represent those people in the younger generation whom Priestley hoped would learn enough from events to accept their responsibilities for other people and build a better world, based on less selfish, more positive values than those of their parents.

> **Key quotation**
>
> 'I remember what he said, how he looked, and what he made me feel.'
>
> (Sheila, H71, L26–27)

Eric Birling

- is immature
- is a drinker
- is weak
- is thoughtless
- is uneasy
- recognises that what he has done is wrong

Eric is described in stage directions as being 'in his early twenties, not quite at ease, half shy, half assertive'. He is the younger brother of Sheila but has a more secretive personality. This becomes understandable when we learn that he is a habitual drinker, the father of what would have been an illegitimate child, a liar and a thief. He is steadily revealed as the black sheep of the family.

He is a young man who does not enjoy a good relationship with his father. Mr Birling does not confide in him about his knighthood, rather choosing Gerald to talk to. Eric is seen by his father as having 'a lot to learn yet' and his view of the world is at odds with his father's; he contradicts Gerald and his father in saying that the workers were not wrong to ask for higher wages, adding 'I'd have let her stay'. While it is clear that Eric has been well educated, having attended a public school and university, Mr Birling clearly thinks that his son has not benefited from this, seeing him as a young and inexperienced boy, unlike Gerald who is already in business and whom he views as a man.

In the first two acts, Eric serves as an irritant to Mr Birling, asking what his father views as silly questions. Eric repeats Mr Birling's views on life in the Inspector's presence, only for Mr Birling to dismiss him ('well we needn't go into all that'), recognising the inappropriateness of expressing his self-interested views now that the Inspector is on the scene.

Eric does not have the same judgement as his father and his drinking may be contributing to his behaviour. Indeed, Eric's hostility and aggression towards his parents grow as the play progresses and as he drinks more. We learn that Eric felt unable to approach his father when he was in trouble and this may explain why he resents his father, and possibly why he drinks so much. We are first made aware of Eric's drinking when he suddenly guffaws in Act One, indicating that he may have known about Gerald's affair. The point at which he laughs is significant, as it gives us a clue as to why he drinks. Eric is disgusted at the hypocrisy of his family and society, but is powerless and unable to redress this because he is at the mercy of the head of the house, his father.

It is only when Sheila reveals, and Gerald confirms, that Eric 'has been steadily drinking too much for the last two years' that we know Eric is a hardened drinker. It is his drinking that Eric says caused him to act so thoughtlessly and brutishly towards Eva Smith, but he feels guilt and regret for his actions (unlike his parents, who continue to deny responsibility): 'And I say the girl's dead and we all helped to kill her.'

Priestley deliberately creates a secretive character in Eric; he appears to be concealing things which later come to light. For example, we may have suspected his guilt when he caught himself in mid-comment, when talking about women's clothes, and when he became uneasy at the Inspector's visit.

It is clear that Eric is immature and this may be why Eva took pity on him, treating him as if he were a 'kid'. She may have recognised in him a need for affection and love. He comes across as a weak and lonely figure, stealing money from his father rather than asking for his help. He is more emotional and demonstrative than any of the other characters, and at the end we see him on the verge of physically attacking his mother: Priestley has him 'almost threatening her' following his fury at her lack of charity: 'my child — your own grandchild — you killed them both — damn you, damn you' (H55).

Like Sheila, Eric takes responsibility for the consequences of his actions, recognising his contribution to the destruction of Eva Smith. We feel that, along with Sheila, he has learned something from the whole affair, unlike the other characters. Eric realises that his parents and Gerald 'may be letting' themselves 'out nicely' but he can't. Unlike them, he can now see that 'It's what happened to the girl and what we all did to her that matters' (H65).

> **Key quotation**
>
> 'It's still the same rotten story whether it's been told to a police inspector or to somebody else.'
>
> (Eric, H64, L36–38)

> **Pause for thought**
>
> Eric is a weak man. Do you think there is sufficient evidence to suggest that he will be able to change his ways, as a result of his experiences in the play?

Gerald Croft

- is confident
- is well mannered
- is a businessman
- is immoral
- is calm
- is conservative

Gerald Croft is described as being 'about thirty' and an 'easy, well-bred young man about town'. He is the son of Sir George and Lady Croft, owners of a rival company to Birling and Co., so he enjoys a privileged position in society and has the self-assurance that comes with this. Gerald has a natural confidence and an authoritative manner which makes that of Mr Birling seem rather forced and artificial.

Gerald is the fiancé of Sheila, and Mr Birling regards him as an ideal son-in-law. Mr Birling sees Gerald's family as socially superior to his own and is happy about the possible merger of the two businesses which may result from his daughter's marriage to Gerald. Gerald is well liked because of this and it is in him that Mr Birling confides about his knighthood. Gerald provides a strong contrast to Eric, Mr Birling's natural son, and Priestley uses him to help show the tensions between Eric and Mr Birling.

Gerald's outlook on life is similar to Mr Birling's and the two of them have experience as businessmen. Gerald agrees with the way Eva Smith's dismissal was handled, telling Mr Birling that 'You couldn't have done anything else'. He appears to have similar business ideas to Mr Birling. In this respect, Gerald has fairly conservative ideas. His vision of the future seems to accord closely with that of Mr Birling.

As with Mr and Mrs Birling, Gerald's first response concerning his part in the affair of the girl is to attempt to conceal it. However, unlike them, he appears to show genuine remorse when the news of her death finally sinks in. While Gerald is immoral in having had an affair and wishing to conceal it from the Inspector, he helped Eva out of genuine concern for her situation. His subsequent affair with her, however predictable, does not appear to have been premeditated.

Key quotation

'I want you to understand that I didn't install her there so that I could make love to her.'

(Gerald, H37, L6–7)

Gerald adheres to traditional ideas about men and women, and, like Mr Birling, he tries to protect Sheila from hearing the news of his affair with Daisy. In some ways this and his reasons for helping Daisy Renton present him as an honourable man.

> **Pause for thought**
>
> Sheila describes Gerald as the 'wonderful Fairy Prince'. Do you think Gerald is an honourable man? Which parts of his actions and words show this?

Gerald did not take advantage of Eva Smith in the violent drunken way in which Eric did and, unlike Eric, he made her genuinely happy for a time. He seems less concerned about status and scandal than Mr Birling, perhaps because his higher social status and more privileged position mean that he does not need to be.

While Gerald is genuinely upset at Eva Smith's death and his contribution to this event, he does not appear to have learnt as much as Sheila or Eric. At the end of the play, it is Gerald who takes charge of matters. He is level-headed and displays the calmest thinking about the identity of the Inspector. He is the first to suggest the Inspector does not exist and to consider a way out for them all. He is the one to telephone the infirmary enquiring about suicides. It is Gerald who first suggests the possibility of there being more than one girl and Mrs Birling is grateful to him for the way he 'argued this very cleverly'. As a result we begin to wonder whether he has any real feelings of remorse.

> **Pause for thought**
>
> Gerald is older than Sheila and Eric but younger than Mr and Mrs Birling. Do you think this accounts for his behaviour and moral attitude? Consider each character's age and Priestley's suggestion that if there is hope for change it will come from the young.

While he admits to having 'kept a girl' the previous summer, he still expects Sheila to accept the engagement ring at the end of the play. His assertion that all is now well places him firmly alongside Mr and Mrs Birling in their hypocritical belief that everything can return to normal again. Now that the Inspector and the dead girl have both been exposed as pretences, he thinks it is acceptable to suggest, 'Everything's all right now, Sheila. What about this ring?' (H71).

Inspector Goole

- is mysterious
- is prophetic
- is calm
- is omniscient (all-knowing)
- is determined
- is Priestley's mouthpiece (voicing Priestley's social and political messages)

The Inspector is a deliberately mysterious figure. At the end of the play we are left wondering who he is or whether he actually exists. We know little about him. He arrives and leaves inexplicably, something the 1954 film of the play exploited well. Even his name leads us to question whether he actually exists. The word 'Goole' suggests his mysterious quality, being a pun on the word 'ghoul'. Is he merely a ghost, someone whose very existence has come about as a result of Eva Smith's death?

Inspector Goole.

TopFoto

Pause for thought

What is your opinion of the Inspector? Who do you think he is? What evidence can you find in the text to support your views?

We might see him as some kind of spirit sent on behalf of the dead girl to torment the consciences of the characters in the play, or perhaps he is some kind of celestial policeman, conducting an inquiry on behalf of God, as a preliminary to the Day of Judgement. Is he an image of conscience — a reminder to us that we are responsible for each other? Priestley deliberately has him enter straight after Mr Birling's claims that there is no such thing as 'community'. The Inspector will present us with an opposing view. During the course of the play he shows how each of the characters contributed to Eva Smith's death and leaves us in no doubt that, despite Mr Birling's beliefs, 'We are members of one body. We are responsible for each other.'

Stephen Daldry's West End production accentuates the moral purpose of the Inspector by presenting him as a time-travelling image of conscience. He not only reminds characters of what they have done but speaks prophetically of the future, referring to 'fire, blood, and anguish'; an allusion to forthcoming wars.

Grade *booster*

It is probable that Priestley did not want to promote any single interpretation of the Inspector. His dramatic power lies in the fact that his real identity is mysterious, unresolved and somehow other-worldly. It is the unresolved tension at the end that makes this play so effective. Recognising that there are multiple interpretations to a text and knowing how the playwright uses characters and events to create effects are signs of a higher-level candidate.

From the moment he enters we are given the impression that the Inspector is different. Priestley describes him as creating an impression of 'massiveness, solidity and purposefulness', indicating his determined and unwavering nature. We are also told that 'He speaks carefully, weightily, and has a disconcerting habit of looking hard at the person he addresses before actually speaking'. While the Inspector is careful to behave correctly, there is an air of menace about his manner which seriously intimidates the others.

The Inspector does not deviate from his moral position and is unwavering in the single-minded way he pursues his chosen line of enquiry. He is confident and commanding, able to control events, and even silences the unstoppable Mr Birling. While the Inspector is actually present, nobody challenges his explanations of events. He has an air of omniscience that Sheila is first to recognise.

The Inspector is able to manipulate characters into revealing things about themselves which they would rather not reveal, or have actually tried to conceal. He acts as a catalyst, making things happen. Sheila sees that there is something about the Inspector which *makes* them tell him things. She recognises that he gives them a feeling that he already knows the truth.

While the name Goole could suggest a spirit-like quality to the Inspector, it may also be a reference to the seaport town of Goole, with the Inspector presented as someone who fishes for information. He is certain of his facts, and leads his enquiry smoothly from one character to the next, revealing the 'chain of events', as he calls it. Priestley has him question characters in a specific sequence, deliberately swapping Eric and Mrs Birling from their chronological order to facilitate the tripping up of Mrs Birling. This contributes to our belief that the Inspector is both an adept questioner and omniscient.

Goole is presented as someone who sees it as his duty to conduct an investigation and he does this thoroughly, making several judgements about characters which the others feel a normal Inspector would not make. Priestley uses the Inspector to expose the fallacy in the characters' claims to be respectable members of society. He is Priestley's mouthpiece, in several respects — in speaking up for the working classes and in representing his strong moral view that change can bring about forgiveness. He is more concerned with morality than law. For this reason, he is harder on those characters who resist telling him the truth.

As a result, he loses patience with Mr Birling and bluntly tells him to shut up: 'Don't stammer and yammer at me again, man. I'm losing all patience with you people.' Because Mrs Birling resists the truth the most, the Inspector is harshest with her.

> **Key quotation**
>
> '…if you're easy with me, I'm easy with you.'
>
> (Inspector, H22, L21)

Text focus

'That doesn't make it any the less yours…in her face.' (H45, L24–32)

The Inspector condemns Mrs Birling for her actions, openly contradicting her statement that it was 'his responsibility'. By saying 'She came to you for help at a time when no woman could have needed it more', he suggests that Mrs Birling has betrayed a fellow woman, and by highlighting her role as a mother with children, he suggests that Mrs Birling is neither a real woman nor a good mother, showing how inhumane she has been. He compounds his criticism of her by appealing to viewers' emotions and by using a list in his statement that 'She needed not only money, but advice, sympathy, friendliness', indicating that all of these things were denied Eva Smith by Mrs Birling. He suggests that Mrs Birling lacks empathy and uses the metaphor of a slammed door to show the cruel treatment that Mrs Birling inflicted on the girl.

Inspector Goole serves several functions in the play. He acts as the storyteller, linking all the separate incidents together into one coherent story. Priestley has him supply dates for events, or fill in background about the girl. He also behaves rather like a priest, someone to whom characters confess their sins, helping them to see the extent of their involvement in the downfall of Eva Smith, and encouraging them to acknowledge their guilt and repent. While the Inspector himself does not hand out forgiveness or punishment, characters are made to recognise that they must find the courage to judge themselves, because only then will they have learnt anything and be able to change themselves.

Eva Smith (Daisy Renton)

- working class
- is a symbol of the need to take responsibility for the consequences of our actions
- is a catalyst for social conscience
- is a good worker
- is poor
- is pretty
- has no family

Eva Smith dominates the action of the play but she is the only character whom we never actually see. Nevertheless, because of what the Inspector and the other characters reveal during the play, we feel that we know her.

She is described by several characters as 'pretty', and to have provoked Sheila's jealousy and attracted both Gerald and Eric she must have been. She is known to have been lively and intelligent, a good worker and about the same age as Sheila. She is poor and working class, and has no parents, relatives or friends, according to the Inspector.

Despite this, and Mrs Birling's prejudice against her, she is shown to have morals. She recognises how foolish it would be to marry a man who does not love her and to accept stolen money, and she appears out of place in the Palace Bar. She is more mature than Eric but does not have his background.

She is presented as a victim, easy prey for those more fortunate than herself. She is accosted by Alderman Meggarty, picked up by both Eric and Gerald, sacked by Mr Birling and as a result of Sheila's jealousy, and refused money and help by Mrs Birling. In some ways, Priestley presents her as a martyr. The lower she sinks in her fortunes, the more honourable and noble she appears.

Priestley uses Eva as a symbol of the common man or woman — he refers to 'the millions and millions and millions of Eva Smiths and John Smiths left with us' and reminds us of our need to take responsibility for our actions and their impact on others. Her connection to the characters in the play is what prompts their confessions. She promotes the idea that we have collective

Pause for thought

The parallels between Eva and Sheila in appearance and age make us question the role luck has in our lives. Had Sheila been born into a less privileged life, would she have suffered the same fate as Eva?

Pause for thought

Eva Smith's identity is immaterial. Consider the way that Priestley's change of her name suggests this and how characters reiterate this point in what they say.

social responsibility, therefore. Despite her lower social class and death, Eva could be said to have the upper hand in the play as she is the one who has shown the others who they really are.

Edna

- is a minor character
- represents the working class
- shows the Birlings' wealth

Edna is a minor character who appears only briefly in the play to serve the Birlings and announce the Inspector's arrival. She is another example of the working class and she helps to create an impression of the Birlings' comfortable lifestyle. In Daldry's production of the play she takes on a more significant role representing the past, present and future. According to Daldry, Edna has always been in the wasteland that surrounds the Birling house. She has seen it all.

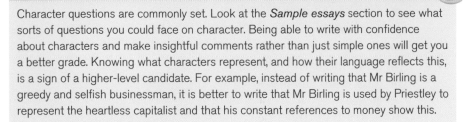

Grade *focus*

Character questions are commonly set. Look at the *Sample essays* section to see what sorts of questions you could face on character. Being able to write with confidence about characters and make insightful comments rather than just simple ones will get you a better grade. Knowing what characters represent, and how their language reflects this, is a sign of a higher-level candidate. For example, instead of writing that Mr Birling is a greedy and selfish businessman, it is better to write that Mr Birling is used by Priestley to represent the heartless capitalist and that his constant references to money show this.

Review your learning

(Answers on p. 85)

1. In what different ways can characters be revealed to us by a playwright?
2. Write down three adjectives (or other terms) to describe Sheila and three to describe Mr Birling.
3. Which characters might be described as self-assured and why?
4. Which characters are working class?
5. List four different functions that the Inspector has in the play?

More interactive questions and answers online.

Themes

- What is a theme?
- What are the main themes in An Inspector Calls?
- How do these themes relate to each other?
- How do these themes relate to characters?

A theme in a text is a key idea that the writer explores. There is no definitive way to identify the themes in any one text and there will be overlaps between themes. However, you can think about key events and characters, the impression left with you at the end of the play and any repeated imagery to help you determine some of the themes in *An Inspector Calls*. Some of the key ideas or themes that Priestley explores in his play are:

- time
- remorse and guilt
- responsibility
- the law and morality
- public image and hypocrisy
- class, status and power
- money

Time

Priestley was fascinated with the subject of time; it appears in a number of his plays, including *I Have Been Here Before, Time and the Conways* and *An Inspector Calls*. Having read P. D. Ouspensky's *A New Model of the Universe*, Priestley used what he learnt in writing *An Inspector Calls*. Ouspensky put forward the idea that when we die we are reborn to the same parents and same circumstances. He suggested that our lives repeat exactly as before time and again, unless we achieve some sort of spiritual enlightenment in our lives which allows us to escape this cycle of repetition and enter a new life, where we do not make the same errors.

Dunne's theory of time also influenced Priestley. This theory was based on the idea that our present, past and future exist at the same time, but we only experience one of these — the present — at any given moment. While all three exist simultaneously, we experience time in a linear way. However, according to Dunne, when we dream we are able to move across these times and are therefore able to see how our past actions have led to our current situation and how they will lead to future consequences. This precognition, which Priestley presents through the reappearance of the Inspector in *An Inspector Calls*, allows people to make decisions concerning their future.

The very fact that a play is written or staged lends itself to different interpretations of time; we can see it as existing in the time it was written, the time it is set and the time it is staged or read. Daldry's production of the play exploits this fascination with time by using a 1912 interior for the Birling house and having the Inspector and the crowd on the street below dressed in 1940s clothes. They reflect back on the past and look forward to the future from the dreamlike wasteland of the exterior.

Time is very important in the play. The Inspector enters at a crucial moment in the play as if he has knowledge of what Mr Birling has said about community. He appears to have foreknowledge of what characters will say and he appears to know what they have done in the past. He makes clear that the characters have a chance to change their ways and thus gain redemption or forgiveness, and he suggests that the world also has this opportunity to learn its lesson. At the end of the play we are given the impression that events will repeat but we may wonder whether they will be different this time round. By having the inspector who is mentioned in Birling's phone call at the end of the play arrive after the events of the play, Priestley allows the characters to reshape their lives and possibly escape the repeated cycle of events. Those who are more spiritually enlightened, such as Sheila and Eric, may do this but we hold little hope for the elder Birlings.

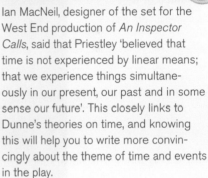

Grade ***booster***

Ian MacNeil, designer of the set for the West End production of *An Inspector Calls*, said that Priestley 'believed that time is not experienced by linear means; that we experience things simultaneously in our present, our past and in some sense our future'. This closely links to Dunne's theories on time, and knowing this will help you to write more convincingly about the theme of time and events in the play.

Remorse and guilt

An Inspector Calls has been seen as a morality play — one that instructs about the condition of man and deals with good and evil. The characters in the play are guilty at various stages of the seven deadly sins — pride, sloth, gluttony, envy, covetousness, lust and anger. The fact that the Inspector asks the characters to reassess their perception of what makes a person a good and respectable citizen, and exposes what appears to be a respectable family to their misdeeds, naturally places the play in a religious context of some sort with the Inspector as a prophetic being. He asks the characters to repent for their sins and to reach spiritual enlightenment. In this respect remorse, a deep sense of regret and guilt for a misdeed, is a theme that Priestley explores.

Remorse is not an emotion which is expressed by every character. However, it is a key theme in the play, which links with Priestley's intentions to create a play in which characters learn something by the end. Different characters react to their guilt differently. Sheila shows great remorse both when she confesses and at the end of the play.

Sheila and Eric.

Eric also expresses a deep sense of guilt when the Inspector recounts what each character did and tells them to remember: 'My God — I'm not likely to forget.' Gerald appears to be remorseful and to regret his actions directly after his confession, when we sense that he feels some guilt in saying, 'She didn't blame me at all. I wish to God she had now. Perhaps I'd feel better about it.' However, he seems to easily forget this, stating that everything's all right once he comes to believe that the Inspector and Eva Smith do not exist.

Similarly, Mr and Mrs Birling do not regret their actions. Mr Birling states that 'There's every excuse for what your mother and I did'; he thinks that they've 'been had' and that Sheila 'will have a good laugh over it' when she understands this.

Responsibility

Closely linked to the theme of remorse is that of responsibility. This is a prevalent theme in many of Priestley's plays, and is a key one in *An Inspector Calls*. Priestley's socialist beliefs inform the play and create a clear message for the audience about an individual's responsibility not just for their own actions but also for the way in which their actions affect others. We first see it indicated in the way that Birling dismisses the 'cranks' who suggest that 'everybody has to look after everybody else'. He refers to society as 'bees in a hive — community and all that nonsense', making clear his view 'that a man has to mind his own business and look after himself and his own.'

> **Key quotation**
>
> **'You'll be able to divide the responsibility between you when I've gone.'**
>
> (Inspector, H54, L24–25)

For Mr Birling, a conservative business owner, looking after himself and his family is all that matters. However, the events of the play, and in particular the arrival of the Inspector, force Birling to see, if only momentarily, his responsibility towards others — the way his actions affect others. The Inspector serves as Priestley's mouthpiece, voicing his views about social responsibility.

> **Key quotation**
>
> **'We don't live alone. We are members of one body. We are responsible for each other.'**
>
> (Inspector, H56, L28–30)

Despite this, Birling refuses to change or take responsibility for the impact he has had on Eva Smith's life. In this he contrasts with his daughter Sheila and (to a lesser extent) his son Eric, who take a more liberal and responsible view of things. They recognise that workers have the right to ask for more money, in the same way that the employers sought higher profits. They can see that Eva and the other factory workers were 'not just cheap labour but people'. They accept that their actions impacted on Eva Smith's life and that they cannot disconnect their actions from the effects these have on others. They recognise that we are all collectively responsible for all that happens in the world. While Mr Birling's primary concern is self-interest, these characters act as the communal conscience of the others.

> **Key quotation**
>
> **'If we were all responsible for everything that happened to everybody we'd had anything to do with, it would be very awkward, wouldn't it?'**
>
> (Mr Birling, H14, L8–11)

> **Pause for thought**
>
> Consider each character's attitude towards responsibility. Who takes most and who takes least responsibility for the consequences of their actions? Find evidence to support your ideas.

The law and morality

The fact that an Inspector calls at the Birlings' house suggests that some legal crime has been committed. Mr Birling's first assumption is that he has come because of 'some trouble about a warrant'. However, as the play progresses we begin to recognise that the Inspector is not simply investigating an illegality— he is investigating immorality.

The difference between the law and morality is a key theme in the play. The Inspector blurs the line between the two. In response to Gerald's statement that 'we're respectable citizens and not criminals', the Inspector says, 'Sometimes there isn't as much difference as you think. Often if it was left to me, I wouldn't know where to draw the line.' This makes clear Priestley's point that, while the Birlings and Gerald may not have committed illegal acts, they have acted immorally and should therefore be held to account.

The only one to have done something illegal is Eric. He initially forced himself on Eva Smith and later stole money.

Text focus

'You're the one it makes *most* difference to. You've confessed to theft…You know.' (Mr Birling, H59, L36–H60, L6)

Mr Birling recognises the difference between the law and morality. He knows that, in stealing, Eric has committed a crime that could lead to an inquest and sentencing, whereas he and the others have simply committed acts which are immoral and as he says may 'perhaps make us look a bit ashamed of ourselves in public' but nothing more. This may explain why Mr Birling thinks he can excuse his and his wife's behaviour: 'There's every excuse for what both your mother and I did — it turned out unfortunately, that's all' (H57).

Public image and hypocrisy

The play is set at a time when public image and respectability were paramount. People in the Edwardian era valued appearances highly. Married couples could have affairs as long as public image and respectability were maintained. Whatever people did that was shameful did not matter as long as no one found out. The elder Birlings and Gerald all try to conceal their actions from the Inspector because of this need to maintain public appearances.

Concern with appearances causes characters to lie and to act hypocritically. Gerald appears to love Sheila, yet he has an affair with Daisy Renton. Mrs Birling presents herself as a respectable citizen, an upstanding member of the community and Brumley Women's Charity Organization, yet she refuses Eva Smith help. Mr Birling presents himself as a family man, yet Eric does not feel that he can go to him for help.

The opening scene suggests a happy celebration among family members but the play reveals that this is all a façade — an appearance. There are tensions between the individuals on stage and they have hidden lives which the Inspector helps to expose.

Pause for thought

Closely related to this theme is the idea of lies. Look through the play. Count the number of times characters lie, either through their actions or in what they say.

The link between public and private becomes evident as events unfold. The characters learn during the course of the play that private behaviour has public consequences, as the Inspector forces them to publicly admit their actions. According to Daldry, his production emphasises this idea of public confession by including a crowd of extras who witness the characters' confessions. When Mrs Birling suggests that the man responsible for Eva's pregnancy ought to be made to 'confess in public his responsibility', she is showing recognition of the power such public humiliation has. However, when she discovers it is her own son who is responsible for Eva's pregnancy she acts hypocritically by not owning up to what she has said.

Mr Birling doesn't want Gerald to know about Eric's and Mrs Birling's actions, for fear this revelation and potential scandal will influence the match between his daughter and Gerald. Public appearance is paramount. Above all Mr Birling fears scandal. His first thought when Eric admits to having stolen the money is to cover it up. When the Inspector leaves, Mr Birling makes clear his views, talking of public scandal and potential threats to his chances of a knighthood.

One of the Inspector's roles in the play is to help characters to develop more honest relationships with themselves, to act less hypocritically — but for some it is obviously too late.

> ### Key quotation
>
> **'They just won't try to understand our position or to see the difference between a lot of stuff like this coming out in private and a downright public scandal.'**
>
> (Mr Birling, H65, L15–18)

Class, status and power

Status or social standing is something that characters in the play value highly. To many it defines their worth as human beings.

Mr Birling recognises the higher social standing of Gerald's family and this, alongside the business benefits his marriage to Sheila will bring, is why Mr Birling likes him. Mrs Birling is described as socially superior to Mr Birling and this may account for their marriage. Both Mr and Mrs Birling hold a relatively high position in society and are very aware of their status, referring to it in an attempt to intimidate the Inspector. Eva Smith, on the other hand, has very little status. She is working class and, as a result, Mrs Birling dismisses her, referring to her as 'the girl' and suggesting that she has no morals or scruples simply because she is working class.

Mr Birling's panic towards the end of the play is rooted entirely in his fear of scandal as this threatens his position in society, and, despite everything that has happened between Gerald and Sheila, he encourages Sheila to accept that a lot of young men have affairs because he recognises the benefits in terms of social standing that the marriage between the two of them will bring.

Characters' status is closely linked to the power that they hold in society. The play concerns itself with the way people exercise power in society. We are shown various forms of power: industrial, physical, emotional, sexual, parental and monetary.

Pause for thought

Consider how the different characters in the play abuse power. Who uses monetary/financial power, for example? Who uses emotional power?

The reasons behind people's abuse of power are also explored. These range from envy, pride, lust and idleness to greed and a desire to feel important. Priestley asks us to to recognise abuses of power and to question the shallow value system focused on status and class. He and the Inspector want us to consider replacing these values with more healthy ones like truth, honesty and compassion.

Money

Money is a key theme in the play which is closely related to class, status and power. It often determines the status of a character and his or her power. It is something that some characters have and others need. Mr Birling is a factory owner who tries to gain maximum profit. His workers strike and try to gain maximum wages but are denied this, and while Mr Birling sees nothing wrong in this, his son Eric recognises its unfairness.

Sheila uses the fact that her family holds an account at Milwards to influence Eva Smith's fate, and Gerald helps Daisy Renton with money. Eric steals money in order to help Eva once he discovers that she is pregnant. The power that money has in the play is evident. Mr Birling's recognition of this power is also clear in his regard for Gerald, the son of a wealthy rival businessman, and in his reaction to Eric's theft and gallivanting.

Priestley asks us to question the value placed on money and to replace it with a more worthy currency — spiritual enlightenment.

Text focus

'You started it. She wanted twenty five shillings a week…You're offering the money at the wrong time.' (H56, L7–13)

In one of his parting speeches the Inspector uses money as a metaphor for loss. He makes clear how little money Eva Smith asked for and was denied, how it was within Mr Birling's power to help her, and how by denying her this help he caused great cost to her and himself. By saying that she paid 'a heavy price' the Inspector uses a pun on the word 'price' because it is not money to which he is now referring but life and death. Further, by suggesting that Mr Birling will 'pay a heavier price still', he indicates that again money has been replaced — this time with guilt. The fact that Mr Birling now offers money, and plenty of it, is both ironic and an indication of how little Mr Birling understands what he has done. As the Inspector points out, it is too late. The currency has changed. What is needed is no longer money, but spiritual enlightenment.

Grade *focus*

Theme questions are commonly set. Look at the *Sample essays* section to see what sorts of questions you could face on theme. Being able to write with confidence about themes and make insightful comments rather than just simple ones will help you get a better grade. For example, rather than simply stating how each character responds to issues of responsibility, you could explore how the theme of responsibility is developed through the character of the Inspector and his role as social conscience and omniscient viewer.

Review your learning

(Answers on p. 85)

1 What is a theme?
2 Make a list of themes that appear in the play and that you have learnt about in this section. Add any further ones you can think of.
3 How is Gerald hypocritical?
4 Who shows most remorse?
5 Who has most status and who has least in the play?

 More interactive questions and answers online.

Style

● **What does style mean?**
● **How has the play been written to be performed?**
● **What sort of language is used in the play?**
● **What examples of imagery are there in the play?**

The style of a text refers to the way in which it is written. It is important to consider how Priestley wrote the play and the choices he made in terms of overall structure, entrances, exits, stage directions, dialogue, language and imagery. This will enable you to understand his intentions and the stagecraft of the play, and help you to write more convincingly about the play in performance.

This section focuses on the following areas to help you understand the style of *An Inspector Calls*:

● structure
  – Greek drama
  – a well-made play
  – detective story
  – morality play
● stage directions
  – sound effects and juxtapositioning
● dramatic and proleptic (anticipated) irony
● realism
● language and imagery

Structure

Most plays are divided into acts and scenes and have come to be analysed using the sections first put forward by Gustav Freytag. His analysis of Greek and Shakespearean drama led him to suggest that plays could be divided into an exposition, rising action, climax, falling action and resolution/denouement.

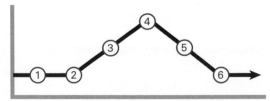

① Exposition — introduction to characters, background, context and themes
② Complication/inciting moment — a problem is introduced
③ Rising action — the plot thickens: more complications and obstacles are presented
④ Climax — the peak moment in the play
⑤ Falling action — things begin to settle
⑥ Resolution/denouement — loose ends are tied up

Some aspects of this structure can be applied to *An Inspector Calls* but so too can other dramatic conventions.

Greek drama

In classical Greek drama, plays conformed to the structure of the **unities**. The three unities of drama were:

- action (plot focuses on one storyline)
- time (stage time and real time are identical and action on stage takes place over no more than 24 hours)
- place (only one setting is used)

An Inspector Calls conforms to the three unities. This means that the action is focused on one storyline; there is only one setting; and the time of action on stage is identical to the real time that the action takes, with the action occurring over less than 24 hours.

Greek drama also involved a chorus, a group of actors who served as narrator. They offered a summary of what had happened so far in the play, a commentary on characters as the play progressed and an explanation about the lessons learned. We can see that Priestley uses a choric device in the Inspector.

In Greek tragedy, the audience also experienced catharsis or a release of feelings which helped to cleanse them, and in Greek drama (both tragedy and comedy) the hero or heroine experienced a significant change in fortune and a discovery or recognition of something previously not known. There was a movement from ignorance to knowledge.

> **Pause for thought**
>
> Can any of the traditions of Greek drama be seen in *An Inspector Calls*?

A well-made play

The **well-made play** is a form of play which was invented by Eugène Scribe. It involves a tightly structured plot and a climax that takes place very close to the end of the story. Most of the story in a well-made play occurs before the action of the play. The action flows smoothly and all the parts of the plot fit together well.

An Inspector Calls has been described as a well-made play. Such plays usually feature:

- an exposition where we are introduced to characters, background and context as well as themes
- carefully timed entrances and exits which help to build suspense
- a secret which is revealed
- carefully timed climactic curtains to end acts
- mistaken identity
- a logical or plausible ending/denouement

Priestley makes use of carefully timed entrances and exits. For example, in Act One the Inspector enters directly after Mr Birling's reference to community. He exits to allow Sheila and Gerald to talk and then enters right at the end of Act One, once we know about Gerald's affair. This is a pattern that Priestley repeats throughout the play.

Pause for thought

Consider the extent to which Priestley uses the conventions of a well-made play in *An Inspector Calls*.

Detective story: 'Whodunnit'

Pause for thought

Do you think Priestley presents us with a traditional whodunnit in *An Inspector Calls*?

A detective story or 'whodunnit' is a story that involves a mystery which is slowly unravelled and eventually solved. It involves a crime, a detective, suspects, clues and eventually a solution. In a traditional whodunnit the criminal is revealed.

Morality play

Some people have classified *An Inspector Calls* as a morality play because such plays (which were performed in the Middle Ages) sought to instruct their audiences how to behave, live and treat others. They were based on opposing the seven deadly sins of pride, sloth, gluttony, envy, covetousness, lust and anger. We can see how these vices are demonstrated by various characters during the play and how the Inspector seeks to instruct them to learn from their mistakes and lead better lives.

Stage directions

The stage directions of a play help to convey an impression of character and to establish the mood of a setting, for the director or producer and ultimately for an audience.

Priestley opens his play with extended stage directions, about both characters and setting. He refers to 'a large suburban house', 'solid furniture' and a 'general effect' that is 'substantial and heavily comfortable'. His intentions are to establish in our minds that the Birling family is relatively well off. He also suggests that 'The lighting should be pink and intimate until the Inspector arrives, and then it should be brighter and harder', indicating that the cosy and close family atmosphere is disrupted by the Inspector's arrival.

Pause for thought

Priestley opens the play in pink lighting. Consider how this might relate to the expression 'rose-tinted glasses'. What could Priestley be saying about those on stage?

Throughout the play, stage directions help to convey a sense of character and atmosphere. Sheila's playful nature and her uneasy relationship with Gerald are seen through the stage directions 'mock aggressiveness' and 'half serious, half playful', and the tensions between Eric and his parents are first hinted at when he 'suddenly guffaws' and 'His parents look at him'. Eric's drunkenness is intimated when he speaks 'rather noisily'. So too we see Mr Birling's misplaced self-assuredness as he is said to laugh 'complacently'. Towards the end of the play, when Gerald calls the infirmary, Priestley indicates the tense atmosphere through stage directions when we are told that 'the others show their nervous tension'.

We gain an impression of how characters are feeling from their actions as indicated in stage directions. Priestley particularly uses adjectives and adverbs to suggest how sections of the play are to be presented. For example, when Mr Birling is being interrogated his mood develops from nervous ('moving *restlessly*') to annoyed ('somewhat *impatiently*') to shocked ('*surprised*') and later disgusted and angry ('staring at the inspector', '*angrily*').

Priestley also conveys information to us at crucial moments through stage directions, for example when Sheila sees the photograph of the girl (H21) or at the end of each of the acts.

Much of the Inspector's character is revealed through stage directions, and his masterful command of the situation, before his final speeches, is suggested through stage direction (H55).

Sound effects and juxtapositioning

Priestley not only uses stage directions to suggest mood and character, he also uses them to indicate key moments. For example, the sharp ring of a doorbell is heard after Birling's speech about community and the door is heard opening and closing at key moments in the play, indicating unseen action and heightening tension.

Priestley also uses juxtapositioning — the placing of contrasting things side by side. He juxtaposes a socialist representative (the Inspector) with someone who has just expressed right-wing views (Mr Birling). He juxtaposes the elder and younger Birlings, and at the end of the play he juxtaposes Mr Birling's confident and sarcastic statement about 'the famous younger generation' who 'can't even take a joke' with a telephone call that threatens once again to prove that the action of the play is anything but a joke.

Dramatic and proleptic (anticipated) irony

Another device at the disposal of playwrights is the use of dramatic irony. The term 'dramatic irony' refers to a situation that arises when the audience knows something that a character or characters on stage do not. There are several instances of this in *An Inspector Calls*. It is especially seen when Mr Birling is delivering speeches early in the play (H6 and 7) to a postwar audience. However, we may also sense some dramatic irony later in the play when the Inspector arrives at the end of Act One, and we know what Gerald has just confessed.

'Proleptic irony' is the term given to a situation which later proves to be ironic. For example, Mrs Birling insists that the father of the child ought to be made to confess his acts (H48), and we later see the irony of this when Eric confesses that he made Eva Smith pregnant. We might also see what Mrs Birling says as dramatically ironic if we have picked up on what the Inspector said earlier (H42 and 43) — 'We do need him here. And if he's not back soon, I shall have to go and find him' — and on Sheila's recognition of the fact that Eric is the father of the unborn child.

When Gerald returns after his walk (H61), this is an example of dramatic irony as we know things about Mrs Birling and Eric that he does not. Some of what Mrs Birling says about Eva Smith, and her disgust at Eva using the name Mrs Birling, can be seen as proleptically ironic, given that Eva Smith was carrying Eric Birling's child and he had asked her to marry him.

Realism

Many view Priestley's play as an example of realism. Its traditionally realistic set and incidents have for many years suggested this. However, Daldry's West End production turns this interpretation of Priestley's play on its head. As Priestley said, 'only a fool would think that I was a realistic dramatist.' The original staging of *An Inspector Calls* in Moscow did not stage the play in a house at all but used a cyclorama — a white canvas wall around the back of the stage which was transformed through lighting. However, its staging in Britain the following year placed the action of the play in a living room, and until Daldry's radical production many stagings followed suit.

Language and imagery

Because of the traditional realism of the stagings, many also view the language of *An Inspector Calls* as realistic. A realistic aspect can certainly be seen in the clear and direct prose that characters use. However, the language of the play reflects its Edwardian setting. The grammatically correct prose of the time seems rather old-fashioned now and does not reflect the sort of language writers use in their works today. Expressions like 'a trifle', 'squiffy' and 'ass' (meaning 'slightly', 'drunk' and 'idiot') are rather dated now. Others, such as 'good sport', 'moonshine', 'By Jingo', 'goggle-eyed' and 'Steady the Buffs', place the play in its setting of 1912.

Despite its apparent realism, the language of the play does carry a metaphorical and dramatic weight. Priestley uses a careful balance of emotive and powerful language, by characters such as the Inspector, Eric and Sheila; euphemism, by the men when talking of taboo subjects; irony, metaphors and imagery. He also uses long and short speeches, monologues, dialogue, as well as dashes and dramatic pauses, short sentences, and carefully placed statements and questions to maintain the audience's interest in a talk-heavy play.

The words of the text serve to do many things. They carry the plot forward, give us an insight into character, suggest themes and help to create mood and tension.

Mr Birling's long monologues at the start of the play, for example, give us an indication of his pompous and misinformed character, whereas Inspector Goole's language is direct, emotive and harsh, suggesting that he is a man who intends to shock the family into recognition of what they have done and is intent on his purpose: 'Burnt her inside out, of course.' His directness and use of emotive words such as 'agony' and 'misery' help to create pity for the unknown girl.

Characters' clipped and interrupted sentences are indicated by Priestley's frequent use of dashes. This helps to suggest the disjointed way characters are speaking.

Euphemism is used in the play when characters refer to taboo subjects, so when Mr Birling talks of Eva becoming a prostitute he talks of her going 'on the street' and Gerald refers to 'women of the town'. Even Eric does not elaborate on his sexual assault on Eva Smith, simply saying, 'that's when it happened.' This contrasts sharply with his later reference to 'fat old tarts': this may indicate his anger and hostility at his parents, but its placement next to his reference to Mr Birling's 'respectable friends' highlights for us the theme of public image and hypocrisy.

Priestley has characters use **irony** in the play, often to indicate a tense atmosphere. The Inspector uses irony, for example in his remark 'Very awkward' (H14) and his comment that he doesn't play golf (H16). His wry sense of humour and jokes at others' expense show that he has the upper hand. Similarly, Gerald and Sheila use irony in their interchange on H34, when she sarcastically refers to 'Buckingham Palace' and being 'engaged to the hero' of the story, and he says 'You're going to be a great help' and 'I'm glad I amuse you'. Here the irony highlights for us the tension between the two of them.

The Inspector's language is made up of short statements, questions and longer speeches, as he prods characters for information, leading them to their confessions. He speaks in a controlled way, often building on

Pause for thought

Look at the way Eric interacts with other characters between H52 and H55. Consider the way Priestley suggests his emotional state through the use of the dash.

comments made by other characters. He repeats words they have used and manipulates them for his own end. Examples include his repetition and manipulation of the word 'impression' on H30; and his manipulation of the word 'position' on H46, the meaning of which he changes from a metaphorical to a more literal one, in order to shock Mrs Birling. He also repeats the word 'offence' with its dual meanings of discourtesy and crime on H31, hinting at the themes of law and public image. His ability to use language in a metaphorical way is seen in his later speeches, which carry almost biblical and prophetic tones. Like a prophet of doom he warns the Birlings that 'if men will not learn that lesson, then they will be taught it in fire, and blood and anguish', metaphorically referring to the forthcoming wars.

Sheila too uses imagery when she talks of her mother's attempts to 'build up a kind of wall', implying the metaphorical distance Mrs Birling creates between classes. When Sheila warns the others that the Inspector is 'giving us rope so that we hang ourselves', she once again uses a metaphor to create a visual image of the way the Inspector skilfully manipulates characters into confessing their sins.

Grade *focus*

Questions on style are not as common as those on character and theme, although stagecraft can be assessed in Edexcel's Literature Controlled Test. It is more likely that you will need to incorporate some material about style into a response in order to meet specific Assessment Objectives. Look at the details relating to AO2 in the *Assessment Objectives and skills* section.

Review your learning

(Answers on p. 85)

1 What traditional five-part structure do plays follow?
2 Name some Greek conventions used in *An Inspector Calls*.
3 What is a well-made play?
4 How would you describe the language the Inspector uses?

More interactive questions and answers online.

Tackling the assessments

- What assessments will you face?
- How will your assessments be marked?
- What sort of questions will you face?
- How can you prepare for your assessment?
- How can you plan your response?
- How can you structure your response?
- How can you ensure the best grade?

Assessments

Depending on which board and specification you are following, you may have to respond to *An Inspector Calls* in an English Literature examination or Controlled Assessment, so knowing the text well is very important. The sort of response you will make in a Controlled Assessment may be written, spoken or multi-modal (a combination of written and spoken).

Whichever board you are studying towards for Literature GCSE, *An Inspector Calls* is an option either as part of your exam or Controlled Assessment. The following table explains which unit the play appears in and gives you information about the sort of question you will be asked and whether you can take your text into the exam or Controlled Assessment.

AQA	Edexcel	WJEC	OCR	CCEA
Unit 1: Modern Prose or Drama exam	Unit 3: Shakespeare and Contemporary Drama Controlled Assessment	Unit 2a: Literary Heritage drama and contemporary prose exam	Unit A662: Modern drama exam	Unit 2: The Study of Drama and Poetry
A written response to one out of two questions based on the whole text	A written, oral or multi-modal response to a question out of a choice on characterisation, stagecraft, theme or relationships	Two written questions on the play: one based on an extract, the other based on the whole text	A written response to one out of a choice of two questions, one of which will be an extract-based question and one of which will be an essay question	A written essay response to one question out of two

AQA	Edexcel	WJEC	OCR	CCEA
Unannotated text allowed	Unannotated text allowed Notes Dictionary or thesaurus Grammar and spelling checker	No text allowed	Unannotated text allowed	Unannotated texts allowed
45 minutes	Up to 2 hours	1 hour	45 minutes	1 hour
30 marks	20 marks	30 marks	27/40 marks Foundation/higher	

Marking

The marking of your responses varies according to the board and the options you or your school have chosen. If you are studying *An Inspector Calls* for examination, an external examiner will mark your response; but if you are responding to it in a Controlled Assessment, your teacher will mark your work and it will then be moderated by someone else. In all cases your ability to respond to the play in a critical way is important. Assessment Objectives for individual assessments are explained in the next main section of the guide (p. 70).

Higher and foundation tiers

All the boards set their English Literature GCSE exams at higher and foundation tiers. If you take the higher tier you can get grades A*–D, with the possibility of an E. If you take the foundation tier you can get grades C–G, with the possibility of a B. You and your teachers (and probably parents) will decide which is the more suitable level for you.

While higher- and foundation-tier questions are similar in content, foundation-tier questions provide students with more guidance — usually in the form of three or four additional bullet points. (Please see the Questions section later in this chapter.)

Essay writing

Whether you are responding in an exam or a Controlled Assessment, knowing how to plan, structure and write an essay is important. You are probably familiar with essay writing so you should have some idea of how to go about it, but the following tips may be helpful:

- Write in the present tense when you analyse texts.
- Only use the past tense when referring to a historical or social fact from the past.
- Address the question immediately.

- Provide evidence for your statements.
- Link your paragraphs.

Essay structure

Essays are made up of three sections: introduction, main body and conclusion.

The **introduction** is made up of three or four sentences directed at the question. You could use the question as a lead and outline the main ideas you will cover in your essay. Look at the following example introduction written in response to a typical AQA question.

> What role does Priestley give the Inspector in the play?

The Inspector serves an important role as the voice of conscience in the play. **1** He is used by Priestley to expose the hypocrisy of the upper classes at the time of the play. He conveys a message of collective social responsibility and asks us to question the part that we play in others' lives. **2**

1 First sentence immediately addressing question

2 Further sentences indicating areas that will be covered in essay

Grade *booster*

Avoid beginning your essay by spelling out exactly what you intend to do ('In this essay I will show that…'): just get on with it.

The **main body** is the central part of the essay and is usually formed of at least three and up to five or six paragraphs. Each paragraph deals with a different point and is linked to the previous paragraph.

The **conclusion** gives your summing up of the evidence and your final words. It should restate main points but throw new light on the subject, rather than just repeat the introduction. An example might be:

By the end of the play Priestley's political message is clear. **1** We and the characters on stage are left in no doubt about the fact that 'we are members of one body'. **2** The omniscient Inspector leaves us with an uncomfortable awareness of the need to accept collective responsibility, so that, by the end of the play, we, like Sheila and Eric, have indeed learnt something. **3**

1 Clear statement concluding essay

2 Second sentence reinforcing opening one and indicating impact of play

3 Final sentence: refers to key theme of essay, linking back to question (Inspector's role); comments on playwright's success in conveying his message, with implied reference to structure of play and the movement from ignorance to knowledge

Grade *booster*

Your entire essay builds an argument based on evidence, like a lawyer in court arguing a case, so writing and structuring your essay well and providing evidence are very important.

Using PEE

When you write a paragraph in a critical essay, you should think of PEE:

- P — Point
- E — Evidence
- E — Explanation

Essentially, you make a statement (or point), you support it with evidence from the text, which may be a quotation, and then you explain how the quotation supports what you said in your statement. It is a good idea to embed your quotation — in other words, to put it into your own sentence — as this is a sign of a higher-level candidate. It is a good idea to link your explanation to the question you are answering, so that you stay on track:

1 The statement (point)

2 The evidence — an embedded quotation

3 The explanation, analysing particular words, explaining how they support the statement, and then linking the essay back to the question. A very good example of using PEE

We are aware of the Inspector's role in the play when he first enters. **1** He is described as creating an impression of 'massiveness, solidity and purposefulness'. **2** By describing him as having 'massiveness' and 'solidity', Priestley shows that he is a character of substance — one with a presence, whose role is important. **3**

Grade *booster*

To check how good you are at embedding quotations, read your sentences out to someone who has not read the play. See if they can tell where Priestley's words begin and end. If not, you've integrated his words smoothly.

Developing an argument and linking paragraphs

Part of essay technique is making sure that the examiner or teacher knows that you are developing an argument. You can make this clear by using **signal words** to signpost your argument.

Word/phrase	What it does
however, although, yet	Suggests an exception: Mr Birling talks of war as being unlikely. However, we recognise the irony in Mr Birling's words.
nevertheless, nonetheless, despite this	Signals a contradiction: Eva Smith is homeless, alone, penniless and pregnant. Despite this, Mrs Birling still believes she has done nothing wrong.
similarly, likewise, in a similar way	Indicates a similarity: Sheila recognises that what she has done is wrong. Similarly, Eric accepts some responsibility for his actions.

Word/phrase	What it does
in contrast, conversely, differs from, while	Suggests a contrast or opposite idea: To Mrs Birling, Eva Smith is immoral, having got herself pregnant. Conversely, Mrs Birling is insistent that she has the moral high ground.
moreover, furthermore, in addition	Builds on the previous point, making a stronger point: She blames Eva Smith and the man who got her pregnant. Moreover, without knowing it, she suggests that the person who should be held responsible is her own son Eric.
above all	Introduces the most important point: Both Mr and Mrs Birling fail to take responsibility for the consequences of their actions. Above all, Mr and Mrs Birling are blind to their failings.
in summary, in conclusion	Concludes the essay: In conclusion, we can see that, while Eric and Sheila appear to have learnt something, the older Birlings have learnt nothing.

Grade *booster*

It is really important that you show an awareness of the play as a constructed work. Make clear that you know this is a play and the characters are constructs through which Priestley expresses his thoughts and ideas. To do this, you need to foreground the playwright. You will gain marks by using statements such as these: Priestley highlights…, illustrates…, makes clear…, reinforces…, elaborates…, shows…, portrays…, demonstrates…

Questions

The questions you will face in your exam and Controlled Assessment could be about characters, themes, structure, the writer's intentions, the play in context or stagecraft. The Controlled Assessment questions are untiered general ones that will be applied to *An Inspector Calls* by your teachers. An example of a question for a Controlled Assessment is:

> *An Inspector Calls* was written and first produced in 1945, and it remains a popular play. Why do you think this is? (Edexcel Literature stagecraft Controlled Assessment)

Examples of questions for an exam are:

> How does Priestley demonstrate the misplaced confidence of the Birlings in their position? (OCR Literature higher-tier exam question)

Compare and contrast the way Birling and the Inspector view society. (OCR Literature higher-tier exam question)

What role does Priestley give the Inspector in the play? (AQA Literature higher-tier exam question)

The Inspector says, 'We don't live alone. We are members of one body.' How does Priestley convey his message of collective social responsibility in the play? (AQA Literature higher-tier exam question)

Look at how Priestley presents Gerald Croft. He is shown to be both selfish and thoughtful in his relationships with Sheila and Eva/Daisy. What is your opinion of him? Give your reasons. In your answer you should consider the language and dramatic devices used in presenting:
- Gerald's treatment of Sheila during the engagement party at the start of Act One
- Gerald's responses to the Inspector about his behaviour towards Eva/Daisy in Act Two
- anything else you think is relevant

(CCEA Literature higher-tier exam question)

Grade *booster*

Many two-part questions ask you to comment on (a) how a character is presented in the passage, then (b) how that character reflects a particular theme. Prepare for these by making sure you know which themes especially relate to each character.

Compare and contrast the way Arthur Birling and Sheila Birling respond to the Inspector's presence and his questions. Look at:
- what they say and do before the Inspector arrives
- what they say and do when they are questioned
- what they say and do after the Inspector leaves

(AQA foundation-tier exam question)

What important role does Priestley give Eric in *An Inspector Calls*? Look closely at:
- what Eric says and does
- other characters' opinions of Eric
- how Priestley describes Eric

(AQA foundation-tier exam question)

In what ways is Eric a more likeable character in Act Three? Remember to support your ideas with details from the play. (OCR foundation-tier exam question)

> For which character in the play do you have the **most** sympathy?
> Give reasons for what you say. (WJEC foundation-tier exam question)

Preparation and planning

Preparing yourself for your assessment will involve a combination of rereading and revision of the text, research, and essay or presentation practise. If you are producing a written response then focusing on writing skills and approaches to questions is important. Choosing the right question is an important part of this. Make sure you choose the question that you are able to answer best. Candidates often find character questions more straightforward than others but there are no set rules. The best thing is for you to get as much practise as possible in the types of questions you might face. This means planning and writing timed essays.

Grade booster

A useful exercise in preparation for your essays is as follows:

1 Write down the key events of the play.

2 Write a one-paragraph description of each of the major characters.

3 Write a brief summary of what the writer set out to do.

Identifying key words and planning ideas

To give shape to your essays, you need to write in a cohesive way. This means that you need to plan and organise your ideas and link your paragraphs.

Whatever question you face, you need to consider what it is asking you. Foundation-tier questions will help you by providing you with some bullet points; but if you are taking the higher-tier GCSE, you won't get much guidance in terms of what areas to explore, so you will need to come up with a planned approach yourself. A good way of doing this is to look at how the question starts and to identify the key words in the question.

Questions often start with words like *What, How, Why* and *Who* but they can start in other ways too. Words like *What* and *Where* suggest straightforward retrieval of information. The word *How* indicates the need to explain and analyse, and the word *Why* suggests that you need to give reasons. Questions that start *To what extent* or *How far do you agree* are asking you for your opinion and setting up a debate. Read the starts of questions carefully to understand what is being asked of you.

Then identify the other key words and consider what each word means and implies. The next step is to come up with ideas of what points you might include in your essay and what events you might refer to. Finally, you need to organise your ideas and decide on the order in which you will cover them.

Consider, for example, the question used earlier:

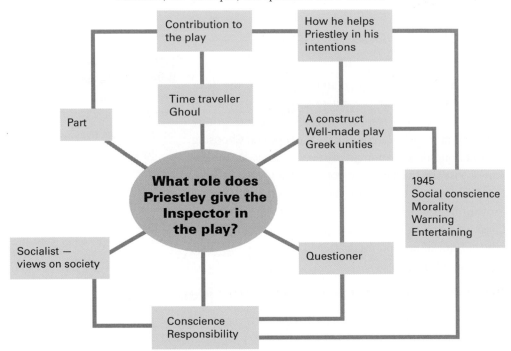

You know that you need to provide information but you can also see that the key words are *role*, *Priestley*, *Inspector* and *play*, so you would then consider each of these words. The word *role* suggests part, contribution to the play, how he helps Priestley in his intentions. The word *Priestley* shows the importance of foregrounding the playwright and remembering that the play is a contruct and the Inspector is a created character serving a purpose, Priestley's. It might also occur to you, therefore, that Priestley was a socialist and had strong views about society. The word *play* suggests the following: on stage, over time, effect on the audience. The word *Inspector* might lead you to Goole/ghoul, one who inspects, questioner, conscience, responsibility, time traveller and so on.

This would give you a number of ideas for different points to make in your essay, for example about the Inspector as:
- a social conscience for the characters and for us
- a questioner exposing the Birlings' hypocrisy
- a ghostly figure or time traveller
- a narrator

- Priestley's voice
- someone who scrutinises family dynamics and the relationship between the individual and society

Your next stage of planning would be to organise these points according to where in your essay you would like them to appear. You might then jot down some events and quotations from the play to support each point. It would also be worth thinking about any play adaptations you have seen and what you know of the context of the play to see if any of this would help you support your points.

If this question were set at foundation tier it could be worded as follows:

> What role does Priestley give the Inspector in the play? Consider:
> - how he makes the characters think and feel about their actions
> - what he says about society
> - why Priestley uses him

If you were answering this question then you would use the bullet points to help guide you but you might also consider some of your own ideas. Remember to find events and quotations from the play to support your ideas. Think also about how the play is performed and the context of the play to help make your answer as good as possible.

An example of a first paragraph in this essay might be:

> It is clear that the Inspector is the voice of conscience, as he arrives shortly after Mr Birling has been selfishly criticising the idea of 'everyone looking after everyone else'. **1** His questioning throughout the play exposes the impact that the Birlings have had on Eva Smith, so that when he talks of the 'millions of Eva Smiths' and 'John Smiths' and says 'We are responsible for each other', we recognise that what he is saying is true. **2** By having the Inspector mention 'fire, and blood and anguish', Priestley uses the fact that the play was written just before the Second World War and is set just before the First World War to suggest that the Inspector is a messenger, warning both the Birlings and the audience of the price they must pay for being collectively irresponsible. **3**

1 A strong topic sentence

2 Evidence and explanation of how Inspector acts as social conscience

3 The point is developed and the candidate introduces the way the playwright uses the Inspector as a voice for his own message of social responsibility to the characters and the audience, expanding the way the word 'conscience' is seen. This sentence also refers to the play's social and historical context. Embedded quotatations are used throughout, helping to make the argument fluid and indicating a higher-level candidate. This is a very good response from an A* candidate.

Oral and multi-modal responses

If you are doing the Edexcel Controlled Assessment and have opted to respond by talking about the play, then you need to make sure that you prepare just as thoroughly as you would do for a written response. You will have plenty of time to research, so use it. The internet is a useful source of information, as is this guide. Follow the advice given previously when thinking about your chosen question. In addition, make sure that you organise your ideas and work out what you will say and how you will support your statements.

Similarly, if you are producing a multi-modal response, using video clips and talking, for example, make sure that you research properly, plan your talk well beforehand, and have everything you need on the day.

Even though you will be presenting information or talking about the play rather than writing about it, you still need to structure what you say and present it in an organised way, using Standard English.

Achieving an A*

In order to gain an A* you have to respond with confidence and enthusiasm, exploring through well-selected quotations how writers use language and structure to create certain effects. You need to show sophisticated critical analysis and originality in your interpretations of the play. You should show how the social and historical context affects how the play was written and is received, and you need to shape your essay well.

Achieving a C

In order to gain a C you need to show understanding and knowledge of how Priestley uses ideas, themes and setting to affect the reader or viewer. You should respond in a personal way to the effects of language and structure and use quotations to support what you say. You should show some awareness of the social and historical context of the play and write clearly.

Review your learning

(Answers on p. 85)

1 What is an essay?

2 How can you plan your answer?

3 How do you use PEE effectively?

4 Which words can you use in an essay to suggest contrast and which to suggest an exception?

 More interactive questions and answers online.

Assessment Objectives and skills

- **What are Assessment Objectives?**
- **Which objectives will I be assessed on?**
- **What skills do I need to meet these objectives?**
- **How can I prepare for these Assessment Objectives?**

A teacher or examiner marks your piece of work based on whether you have fulfilled certain Assessment Objectives (AOs). In other words, they mark your work to see whether you have done certain things. The key AOs that apply to your English Literature studies of *An Inspector Calls* are as follows:

- AO1
  - Respond to texts critically and imaginatively.
  - Select and evaluate relevant textual detail to illustrate and support interpretations.
- AO2
  - Explain how language structure and form contribute to writers' presentation of ideas, themes and settings.
- AO4
  - Relate texts to their social, cultural and historical contexts.
  - Explain how texts have been influential and significant to self and other readers in different contexts and at different times.

The importance of each of these AOs varies across boards.

- Edexcel only assesses AO1 in its Controlled Assessment for *An Inspector Calls*.
- WJEC places more weighting on AO4 and AO1 than AO2 in its exam.
- CCEA places more weight on AO1 and AO2 than it does on AO4 in its exam.
- AQA places equal importance on AO1 and AO2 but less on AO4 in its exam.
- OCR places equal importance on AO1 and AO2 in its exam.

Let's break down each AO to see what it means.

AO1

'Respond to texts *critically*': this means that you say what you think of the play and explain why you think this. You are being asked to *analyse* the text as a piece of literature that has been created by a writer. Being able to discuss how Priestley creates characters through a combination of what characters say and do, how they speak and stage directions would show that you are looking at the play in a critical way. Discussing the way Priestley creates tension in the play would show that you are analysing how the play works.

'...and *imaginatively*': this means you do not simply repeat straight-forward ideas. You need to know the text well enough to come up with your own interesting interpretations. Knowing, for example, that Sheila and Eva are similar in character and appearance but that one is born into a middle-class family and the other is poor could lead you to suggest that the play invites us to ask questions about the fairness of class distinctions, Mrs Birling's prejudices and the nature of luck or fate. This would show that you had thought imaginatively about the play.

'*Select* and *evaluate* relevant textual detail to illustrate and support interpretations': this means that you can find words, phrases and evidence from the play to support the comments that you make. You are also able to explain the choices the writer has made and *assess* how effective you think they are in contributing to the writer's intentions. For example, at the end of the play Gerald says to Sheila, 'Everything's alright now, Sheila. What about this ring?' — you might use this as evidence that he has learnt nothing, and is happy to return to things as they were at the start. You might evaluate Sheila's ambivalent answer, 'No, not yet. It's too soon', as contradicting her otherwise clear recognition that things are different now. She appeared to have learnt something and to have changed but she sounds uncertain here. Perhaps Priestley is suggesting that for her, a young woman in 1912, despite her personal beliefs, there is no way out? Another example might be Priestley's repeated statement of 'it frightens me', which both Eric and Sheila say. This repetition of a key phrase helps viewers to speculate about what it is the younger generation fear. Could it be that Priestley is making a statement about humanity's innate selfishness, our inability to learn or to care about another, or perhaps the futility or shallowness of life?

AO2

'*Explain how* language structure and form contribute to writers' presentation of ideas, themes and settings': this means you show how the words

Priestley uses and the way he has shaped and organised his play have helped him to convey certain ideas, messages and a setting. This area is covered closely in the *Style* section of the guide. You might discuss the way the Inspector's parting speeches elucidate the theme of collective responsibility, for example.

AO4

'*Relate* texts to their social, cultural and historical contexts': this means that you use your knowledge about the time in which Priestley wrote and set the play. For example, you show that you understand the attitudes towards class in 1945 and 1912 and how these relate to events in the play and the way characters behave. Your knowledge of the events of the First World War and how they make Birling's speeches dramatically ironic is also relevant to this AO. This is covered extensively in the *Context* section of the guide.

'*Explain how* texts have been influential and significant to self and other readers in different contexts and at different times': this means that you can show how you have responded personally to the play and how the play still holds meaning for you and for others. In other words, you can explain how it is still relevant today and has been and would be relevant at different times throughout history. For example, the play can still be seen as relevant because it deals with issues that we still face, such as status and power. In fact it is even more relevant now, given the commercialism of the modern world. The self-interested views that Mr Birling expresses when he describes community as 'nonsense' would have been particularly relevant in the 1980s when the then prime minister Margaret Thatcher claimed that there was no such thing as society.

Grade *booster*

Make sure you write the names of the play and characters correctly. Also use quotation marks around the name of the play and words taken from the text.

How you can prepare

Getting to know the play well is the best way for you to prepare to meet these AOs. Finding out exactly what is required of you in the exam or Controlled Assessment will also help. Regardless of whether you are studying *An Inspector Calls* for exam or Controlled Assessment, understanding the play properly and being able to discuss key ideas in detail will help you. Being able to support your comments and explore how Priestley creates meaning and effects is essential. Reading around the subject and looking into the background of the play, for example what was happening in 1912 and 1945, will also help you. The *Contexts* section of this book is very useful for this. Going to see a production of the play is also very beneficial.

Before you complete your assessment, make sure you look at plenty of example questions and attempt some. Remind yourself of the key AOs and make sure you know how to address them. Read the *Tackling the assessments* and *Sample essays* sections in this book. Ask your teacher for help if you need to.

Grade *booster*

Make sure you write in an appropriate way in your exam. Although it is your understanding of the play and not the way you write that is being assessed, you must write clearly and formally.

- Do not use slang or colloquial language, except when you are quoting from the play: for example, don't write *Eric's a bit of a git really.*

- Use appropriate critical vocabulary: words like *convey, portray, demonstrate, devices* and *technique* are examples.

What you will not get marks for

The AOs guide you towards what you need to write. They tell you what you will gain marks for. It is important to know that you will *not* get marks for the following:

- **Retelling the story.** Examiners already know what *An Inspector Calls* is about. You will not gain any credit for telling them what they already know and what they assume you already know. You must answer the question you are asked and address the AOs, not write down everything you know about the story — that would be a waste of your time.

- **Using very long quotations.** You need to quote from the play to support what you write, but quoting long sections will not gain you marks. It wastes your time and just shows that you are not able to select the quotation you need. It's much better to quote short phrases and words or to embed quotations into your sentences.

- **Giving your opinion in a dismissive way without any support.** The examiner wants to see that you have responded personally to a text so writing your opinion is a good thing, but only if it makes sense and you have supported what you write with evidence from the text or elsewhere. Rather than writing *Mr Birling's a stupid old man*, write *When Mr Birling says that war is impossible and the Titanic is unsinkable, he is making statements that show that he is ill-informed about current events and misjudges future ones.*

- **Identifying features.** It is good if you are able to recognise when a character is using a metaphor or being sarcastic or when there is tension in the play, but it is not enough just to recognise these features. You shouldn't just write: *Sheila uses the metaphor of a wall when she talks to Mrs Birling.* You need to be able to explain why Priestley uses these devices and how they work in creating certain effects, so you should write: *Priestley uses a metaphor when Sheila says 'You mustn't try to build up a kind of wall' to suggest the way Mrs Birling is distancing herself from Eva Smith and other working-class people. He creates a visual image of something that can and will be easily destroyed by the Inspector's questions.*

Review your learning

(Answers on p. 86)

❶ What AOs will you be assessed on for English Literature?

❷ Give two examples of something that would not get you marks.

❸ Give an example of how you would show that *An Inspector Calls* is still influential to readers.

More interactive questions and answers online.

Sample essays

- **What does the beginning of an essay look like?**
- **How do I write a character essay?**
- **How do I write a theme-based essay?**
- **What makes a good essay?**

Essay questions and some samples are provided in the *Tackling the assessments* section of this book. Below you will find some more extracts from sample essays, with examiner comments.

Look at the C-grade responses and try to improve these. Then look at the A-grade responses and compare them to your own ideas. Although there is no set way of approaching an answer, the higher-level responses will guide you in answering questions yourself.

Essay beginnings

Remember to begin your essay by immediately focusing on the question. You should use the question as a lead and outline the main ideas you will cover in your essay. This was covered in the *Tackling the assessments* section, so refer back for more guidance.

> How does Priestley use the character of the Inspector to expose tensions in the Birling family? (AQA Literature)

For this sort of question you will have had plenty of time to research and up to 2 hours to respond, so a thorough response will be expected. If you choose to respond in writing, then you need to take your lead from the set question.

Grade C response — beginning

I'm going to write about how the Inspector exposes tensions in the Birling family. **1** He does this because he is organised in his line of enquiry and deals with one character at a time. **2** Each time he asks characters questions, he knows what the character will say and has the power to make them say things that show their guilt. **3**

1 Immediate focus on question, but says what will be done rather than just doing it

2 Knowledge of Inspector's approach is shown, but link to question is not clear

3 Shows knowledge but does not refer to evidence, and does not link ideas back to question or explain how they show tension

This response is a C-grade one because understanding and knowledge of the play are shown by the candidate and these are focused on the question, at first. However, statements *imply* understanding of how tension is created rather than *show* it, and evidence is needed. Furthermore, although the answer starts quite well and is focused on the question, it is not advisable to say what you will do, and the second and third sentences do not clearly link to the question.

Grade A response — beginning

The Inspector is a device used by Priestley to expose not only tensions in the Birling family but also flaws within individuals and society. **1** The Inspector's role is to act as a beacon of light exposing the family to scrutiny, as opening stage directions state that upon his arrival the 'pink and intimate' lighting of the scene should become 'brighter and harder'. This suggests that the family will be placed in the spotlight and will have to face the truth about their hidden lives. **2** It is the Inspector's questioning and characters' reactions and revelations that expose the tensions between family members. **3**

1 Immediate focus on question; shows understanding of Inspector's role and of Priestley's deliberate creation of this role

2 Use of PEE to show how Priestley uses stage directions to indicate Inspector's role in creating tension

3 Explains how structural choices made by Priestley, such as what the Inspector says and how and what characters say and do, help to expose tensions. This gives an idea of what the essay will cover.

This response is an A-grade one because of the confidence with which the candidate writes about the play and the way the paragraph is very clearly linked to the question. Understanding and interpretation of the play are shown by the candidate and s/he has referred to well-selected evidence and embedded quotations. The candidate's awareness of Priestley as a writer is clear from the explanation of how he uses structural and presentational devices to show family tensions.

This candidate continued in this very focused way when discussing tensions between Eric and his father, in the next paragraph:

4 A point is made; repetition of the word 'tension' makes link to first paragraph

5 Gives evidence, then explains how this shows tensions between father and son. Good use of PEE

We see indications of this tension **4** when the Inspector is first mentioned. Gerald and Mr Birling share a joke at Eric's expense which Eric takes exception to, and we see Eric described as 'uneasy' — suggesting that he and his father do not get on and there is something he is hiding. **5**

Character questions

Character questions are common in assessments and some students find these easier to do. Be prepared to answer a question that asks you to consider the following:

- **The importance of one of the characters.** For this sort of question think about what the character does and what this may show about others. Think also about how they help the plot. What role do they have? Think what would happen if they weren't included. Consider whether they represent a certain point of view. Are they a symbol of something important?

- **Whether a character has changed or developed during the play.** For this sort of question think about how Priestley has created the character. Is the character described differently, or acting or speaking differently, at various stages? For example, Sheila is seen as selfish at the start but she acts very differently at the end of the play. Do the character's thoughts reflect a change?

- **Whether a character has learnt anything by the end of the play.** For this use a similar thought process to the one described in the previous point.

- **Similarities or differences between characters in the play.** For this, think about how Priestley has created the characters. Draw up a table to compare and contrast them. Think about why Priestley has included this comparison — what point is he making? For example, contrasts between Eric and Gerald exaggerate the tensions between Eric and his father.

- **Whether a character is appealing or likeable.** For this think about how Priestley has created the character. Look at the sort of words he used to describe the character. Look at stage directions, at verbs, adjectives and adverbs used for the character. 'Sneered' has a stronger meaning than 'laughed'. It would distance us from the character. The way Priestley presents the character will give you an idea of whether he wants us to like the character.

- **Whether we sympathise with a character.** For this, do the same as in the previous point, but also look at events and a character's response to events during the course of the play. Perhaps the character changes and, as a result, our response to them changes too.

- **How the writer shapes a character.** For this think back to all the aspects discussed in the *Characterisation* section of this book.

- **How the writer wants us to react to a character.** For this, consider how Priestley has shaped the character and whether the character changes or develops.

An example of a character question is:

Look at how Priestley presents Gerald Croft. He is shown to be both selfish and thoughtful in his relationships with Sheila and Eva/Daisy. What is your opinion of him? Give your reasons.
In your answer you should consider the language and dramatic devices used in presenting:

- Gerald's treatment of Sheila during the engagement party at the start of Act One
- Gerald's responses to the Inspector about his behaviour towards Eva/Daisy in Act Two
- anything else you think is relevant

(CCEA Literature higher-tier exam question)

Grade C response

The way that Gerald treats Sheila during the engagement party at the beginning of Act One shows that he is kind to her on the outside, but also lying to her on the inside. **1** He produces a ring for her and flirts with her, saying he has been trying to be part of the family for a long time. **2** However, he also says that he was busy at the works when we find out later this was not true. **3** He is protecting himself and trying to make a good business marriage rather than demonstrating real love. **4**

1 Clear focus on question; use of the bullet points to structure response

2 Evidence provided, but lack of direct quotation from text

3 More evidence provided but no quotation

4 Makes valid points but does not elaborate or explain them in sufficient detail to warrant more than a C grade

Grade A response

1 Clear focus on question; shows awareness of Priestley as a writer and Gerald as a constructed character

2 PE: point and evidence are provided, through embedded quotations

3 E: explanation is provided

4 Previous point is reinforced, again using PEE

5 Development of point and strong concluding sentence

6 A new point is introduced, and evidence provided and analysed. Stage directions as well as what characters say are considered.

Gerald is presented as a strange mix of selfishness and thoughtfulness. **1** He appears to genuinely care for Sheila; at the engagement party he says that he wants to make her 'as happy as' she 'deserve(s) to be', but we later discover that he has been concealing an affair from her. **2** This shows that he is not being his true self with her. **3** While the two of them joke with one another, which could suggest they are happy, it also suggests that Sheila is not entirely at ease with Gerald. For example, she raises the issue of his not spending time with her the previous summer in a joking way, rather than in private and seriously, **4** and Gerald's response is dismissive: 'And I've told you — I was awfully busy at the works all that time.' It is evident this is a sticking point and that there are tensions between the two of them. **5**

Gerald is thoughtful in surprising Sheila with an engagement ring: Priestley writes 'He produces a ring case' and Sheila is described as 'excited', showing her happiness. However, the ring is the one he has chosen — '…is it the one you wanted me to have?' — which indicates his selfishness. He also ruins a normally private moment by producing the ring in public and seems to be congratulating himself when he smiles in giving it to her. **6**

He does not respond to Sheila's kiss of thanks, and says nothing more to her before she exits, focusing more on Mr Birling's speech when he says, 'I believe you're right, sir.'**7** This could suggest that his and Sheila's is to be a marriage of convenience, built around selfish business motives rather than thoughtful ones.**8**

Theme questions

Some questions focus on themes. You might get a question that asks you to consider one of the following:

- **The presentation of a theme in the play.** For this, you need to look at the different ways used by Priestley to present the theme — for example through key events, through particular characters, through language and imagery and through the ending.
- **How the theme influences events in the play.** For this, consider how things would have been different if, for example, the theme of collective responsibility was not covered or money was not an issue in *An Inspector Calls*. Think about which characters or events in the text are shaped by the theme.
- **How a theme is evident through the behaviour of one or more characters.** Think, for example, about how the theme of collective responsibility is apparent through the Inspector's behaviour.
- **How the importance of a theme is evident.** For this, look back at the section on themes and remind yourself of how we become aware of them.

An example of a theme-based question is:

The play focuses on the difference between public and private behaviour. Explain. (AQA higher-tier exam question)

This question is about the theme of public image and hypocrisy (as discussed in the *Themes* section of this book).

Grade C response

Many characters in the play behave in a way to show that they are different in private than public.**1** One character who does this is Gerald. He has an affair with Daisy even though he is engaged to Sheila and is celebrating his engagement to her.**2** Another character who behaves differently in public and private is Mrs Birling. She pretends to be an upright person but she refused to help Eva when she came to her for help: 'I was perfectly justified in advising my committee not to allow her claim for assistance.'**3** Mr Birling goes on about his knighthood and thinks appearances are important.**4**

7 A further point and evidence

8 All points are brought together in the analysis to form a concluding statement about the nature of Sheila and Gerald's relationship and how this shows Gerald's selfishness, linking back to the question asked. This is an A-grade response.

1 Strong focus on question, but clumsily worded

2 An example of the difference between public and private behaviour with evidence but no explanation

3 Another example of the difference between public and private behaviour with evidence, and quotation but no explanation

4 A loosely worded sentence which sounds vague

1 Strong focus on question, with indication of how Priestley shows the difference between public and private behaviour

2 Clear development of first point

3 Analysis of why Priestley is able to show the difference between public and private behaviour. Awareness of choices made by the playwright and strong focus on key words in the question — 'private' and 'public'

4 Further point showing awareness of devices used by playwright

5 Evidence provided

6 Explanation of evidence

Grade A response

The difference between public and private behaviour is explored in the play in the way that Priestley contrasts the impression we first gain of characters with their true selves. **1** We discover that characters have hidden lives based around lies. **2** This exposure of lies happens because an outsider, the Inspector, interrupts a private celebration, the engagement party, and forces the characters to confess their actions publicly. **3** The Inspector is used by Priestley as a device; he manipulates characters into confessing their lies. **4** His knowingness is a tool that facilitates this exposure, so that when he says 'I think you remember Eva Smith now, don't you, Mr Birling?' after Mr Birling's initial denial, we begin to see a pattern that repeats itself throughout the play. **5** Priestley uses the omniscience of the Inspector to help him break down the 'wall' that characters try to build between themselves and others — a wall which distances them from others and which serves to protect them from public exposure. **6**

Other questions

You could face other kinds of questions, for example on productions, stagecraft or structure. You can find extracts of responses online. Here's an extract from a response to a question on productions of the play. Read the examiner comments to help you understand how to write a good response.

> Remind yourself of events from the Inspector's exit in Act 3 to the end of the play. Consider how this section of the play is shown in two productions (either film or stage). By referring closely to Priestley's text, explore how the characters' reactions to the Inspector are portrayed in the film/stage versions you have watched.
> You should consider:
> • the thoughts and feelings that the characters express
> • the way the characters behave
> • the dramatic effect of the scene
> (Edexcel Controlled Assessment)

For this sort of question you will have had plenty of time to research and up to 2 hours to respond, so a thorough response will be expected. If you choose to respond in writing, then you need to take your lead from the set question.

Grade C response

In the West End production of the play, the director suggests that this is a key moment in the play through music, lighting and special effects. **1** The Inspector is presented as a time traveller and his importance is highlighted through the dramatic music that accompanies his exit. **2** Also when Sheila is left on stage she spends a few moments on her own. **3** The 1954 film version of the play treats this section of the play differently. **4** The Inspector is kept in a room next to the dining room while the characters discuss events and then he just disappears. This shows his mysterious nature. **5**

1 Does not clearly relate to question

2 Focuses more on question and starts to look at presentational devices and the impact, but statements are not fully explained (e.g. that the Inspector is a time traveller)

3 The significance of Sheila being alone on stage is not explored — so shows implied rather than explicit understanding

4 Another version is cited and contrasts suggested

5 Some understanding of a different interpretation and its effects is apparent.

Grade A response

In Daldry's stage production of this section of the play *An Inspector Calls*, the director accentuates the characters' reactions to the Inspector by having the Birling house collapse. **1** The house is presented as a character responding to the Inspector's will and symbolically collapsing when the Birlings' lies are revealed. **2** Dramatic music and flashing lights suggest the symbolism of the moment and its relation to events in history, such as the collapse of buildings during the Second World War and the collapse of capitalism. **3** When the Inspector has left the stage, Daldry allows Sheila a few moments to react. This interpretation of the play highlights Priestley's intentions — to show the impact the Inspector has had on Sheila. **4** It indicates that she may recognise the significance of what has happened, even if none of the others have. **5** In contrast, **6** the 1954 film version of the play does not have the Inspector leave until the very end. Instead the Birlings and Gerald are presented discussing the Inspector's identity while he sits in a room next door. **7** This is a convenient device which allows the director to play on the mysterious nature of Inspector Goole, the very subject under discussion in the next room. **8**

1 Clearly relates to question

2 Develops first point by analysing effect of choices made by director and how these relate to Priestley's intentions

3 Link to social and historical context

4 Again, evaluation of how choices show writer's intentions

5 Explanation of how this interpretation works

6 Comparison with a different source is clearly signalled

7 Understanding of a different presentation is shown

8 Its effects are explored, and awareness of the writer and director are apparent

Here is a question on our reactions to Eva Smith. Although this is a foundation-tier question, with bullet points to guide you, both grade C and grade A responses with examiner comments have been provided to help you.

> How does Priestley create sympathy for Eva Smith in the play?
> Consider:
> • what the Inspector says
> • characters' reactions to events
> • the way Eva Smith is presented
> (AQA)

Grade C response

Priestley creates sympathy for Eva Smith by showing how badly she was treated by the other characters and that she did all she could to improve her situation but bad things kept happening to her. She is seen as a victim who is badly treated by others. **1**

We feel sorry for Eva Smith because she is poor and has no friends or family. The Inspector tells us this when he says, 'she was alone, friendless, almost penniless'. He describes her as 'desperate' and this makes us have sympathy for her. **2**

The way Eva died also makes us feel sorry for her as it is a horrible way to die. **3** 'Burnt her inside out, of course.' You would have to be really desperate to do that. **4**

When the Inspector goes through the way all the characters treated her we feel sad because we realise how Gerald and Eric used her and how the others used their power to abuse her. All of this must have made her feel very alone. **5**

Overall lots of good points covering AO1, some coverage of AO2 and none of AO4. This is a strong C candidate and could be a B depending on the remainder of the essay.

Grade A response

Eva Smith is used by Priestley as a symbol of the working class. **1** During the play she is presented as a victim of circumstance and this in itself provokes our sympathy, but alongside this Priestley uses the character of the Inspector to evoke even more sympathy. **2** He details the way in which each character has contributed to Eva Smith's demise and describes the horror of her death in an emotive way. **3**

Priestley through the Inspector continually refers to Eva Smith as a 'young woman', suggesting her vulnerability. This creates sympathy for her, as we recognise how helpless a character she is. This is accentuated because Priestley presents her as having no family or friends. Her social isolation exacerbates her vulnerability and heightens our sympathies for her. The Inspector also talks of her death in emotive ways, referring to her 'agony' multiple times, again creating sympathy for her. **4**

The Inspector's first reference to her suicide is graphic in its description: 'she'd swallowed a lot of strong disinfectant. Burnt her inside out, of course.' Its purpose is to shock. Eric's involuntary 'My God!' and his father's 'Horrid business' demonstrate the impact these emotive words have on characters, **5** but the dismissive way in which Mr Birling reacts, saying 'But I don't understand why you should come here, Inspector', introduces the contrast between father's and son's attitudes to community and Mr Birling's inherently selfish attitude to events. This

---

1 Good start, focused clearly on the question and indicating areas which will be explored

2 Good point in the first sentence with some evidence (PE), but no explanation of this quotation. Instead another quotation is supplied and analysed. An opportunity is missed here but it is still a good paragraph.

3 Good opening sentence

4 Quotation with some explanation which is a personal response, but does not look at use of language, so AO2 is not addressed

5 Good point with evidence and some reinforcement, but again AO2 is not addressed

---

1 Opening sentence foregrounds the playwright and shows awareness of Eva as a construct — very good on AO1

2 Clear focus on question with indication of main device used by playwright (Inspector)

3 Focus on structural and language choices made by writer, indicating that the essay will cover AO2

4 Well-written paragraph using PEE, strong critical vocabulary and focus on question

5 PEE and AO2 are addressed

helps to create even greater sympathy for Eva Smith as she is presented as someone whom others can readily dismiss.**6**

This easy dismissal of Eva Smith is later seen when Mrs Birling refers to her as 'the girl' and 'girls of that class', insinuating a moral distance between herself and Eva Smith. By presenting both Mr Birling and Mrs Birling as dislikeable characters who are arrogant and lacking in compassion, and having them dismiss Eva Smith, we are naturally drawn towards her as we recognise the unfair way she is treated by others. She is presented as a victim undeserving of her ill treatment.**7**

This unfair treatment is detailed for us by the Inspector, who carefully presents us with each character's contribution to Eva Smith's life from Mr Birling's firing of her through to her becoming pregnant by Eric.**8** He uses careful and targeted questioning to lead us step by step through the chain of events so that, even though Eva Smith is not present on stage, it is as if we are experiencing events as they happen.**9**

Her physical absence from the stage and her two names help to reinforce the idea that Eva Smith is a symbol of many women of her class.**10** Priestley deliberately has the Inspector liken her to others of her class by saying, 'Like a lot of these young women…', and in his parting speech he groups her with others by referring to the 'millions and millions and millions of Eva Smiths and John Smiths', making clear that she represents all those who have suffered as a result of their position in society and others' refusal to take collective social responsibility.**11** Here and elsewhere Priestley has the Inspector use repetition, lists and antithesis to create a lasting memory of Eva Smith's situation. By doing this Priestley hopes we will not forget 'their lives, their hopes and fears, their suffering and chance of happiness'.**12**

This has all the necessary elements of an excellent response and indicates a strong candidate working to at least A-grade standard.

6 Awareness of themes related to Eva Smith, showing strong focus on AO2; clear reference to sympathy, linking back to question; good link to next paragraph

7 PEE with very good analysis and link back to question. Good concluding sentence linking to next paragraph

8 Well-made point with evidence

9 Strong focus on AO2

10 Focus on AO2 and AO4

11 PEE and focus on AO4

12 Use of PEE and focus on AO2

Review your learning

(Answers on p. 86)
1. What sort of character questions might you face?
2. What sort of theme questions could you face?
3. What is the best way to start an essay?
4. If your understanding is implied rather than made clear, which grade are you likely to get — a C or a B?

More interactive questions and answers online.

Answers

This section provides answers to the 'Review your learning' questions from each of the earlier sections.

Introduction (p. 7)

1 Setting, characters, themes, style, context.
2 Use techniques that work for you; reread the play; know key points.
3 Sit at a table; revise for 40-minute periods; take ten-minute breaks; reward yourself for hard work; have a learning manager to test you; colour-code your text into key areas.
4 The set design is radical. Daldry presents the action of the play in a 1912 house on stilts, in a rainy wasteland of 1945. The Inspector is a ghostly time traveller forcing the Birlings to come out of their safe environment into the landscape below, which appears to be war-torn Britain but could be any wasteland that has come about as a result of man's irresponsibility to fellow man. The combination of time settings in this production is radical and helps to create the effect that it is not only the Inspector but history itself that judges the Birlings.

Context (p. 15)

1 The circumstances at the time the text was written.
2 His home town, his work in a wool mill, his fascination with time.
3 Class structure, strikes, the *Titanic*, upcoming wars.
4 Changes in class structure and attitudes to women, changed attitudes to responsibility and politics.

Plot and structure (p. 28)

1 Birling and Gerald agree there was no other choice — she had to go. Eric thinks that it's unfair and that she was entitled to ask for higher wages.
2 Gerald's
3 She used her influence as a prominent member of Brumley Women's Charity Organization to refuse her help.
4 No Inspector Goole exists in the police force. It makes them think about an escape from taking responsibility for their actions.

Characterisation (p. 43)

1 Stage directions, what characters say and do, how they speak, what others say and think about them, what they think themselves.
2 Sheila: self-centred, jealous, remorseful. Mr Birling: smug, opinionated, social climber.
3 Mrs Birling and Gerald, because they are of a higher class than the others.
4 Eva Smith and Edna.
5 Priestley's mouthpiece, priest listening to characters' sins, conscience, links the stories.

Themes (p. 51)

1 Key idea in a text.
2 Public image and hypocrisy, money, time, power and class, law and morality, regret and guilt, lies and deceit, old and young, gender, love, responsibility.
3 He has an affair while being involved with Sheila.
4 Sheila.
5 Gerald: most; Eva: least.

Style (p. 58)

1 Exposition, rising action, climax, falling action, resolution.
2 Chorus; three unities of time, place and action; characters learn something by the end; emotions purged (audience — guilt).
3 A play with a tightly woven plot, a climax very near the end, and the bulk of the story occurring before the play begins.
4 Prophetic, emotive, direct and powerful.

Tackling the assessments (p. 69)

1 An organised piece of writing made up of introduction, main body and conclusion. It develops an argument and gives supporting evidence.
2 Identify and brainstorm key words; make a list of points; find evidence to support points.
3 P — point, E — evidence, E — explanation. Make a statement, support it with evidence, and explain how the evidence shows what you said in your statement.
4 For contrast: in contrast, conversely, while. For an exception: however, although, yet.

Assessment Objectives and skills (p. 74)

1 AO1, AO2, AO4.
2 Using long quotations; retelling the story.
3 The world is a materialistic place and people's standing in society is often based on material wealth. The play asks us to reassess these judgements.

Sample essays (p. 83)

1 The importance of a character; whether a character has changed/developed or learnt anything during the play; whether we sympathise with a character; how the writer shapes a character; how the writer wants us to react to a character; similarities/differences between characters.
2 The presentation of a theme; how the theme influences events; how a theme is evident through characters; how the importance of a theme is seen.
3 Immediately focus on the question.
4 C grade.

Notes

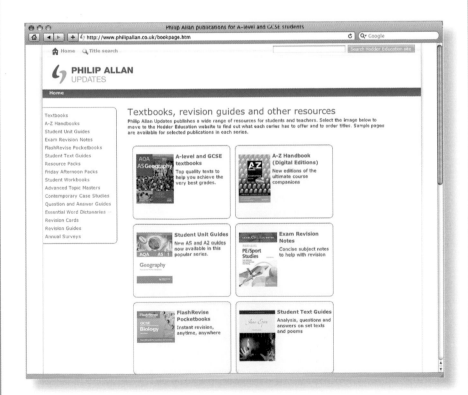

Go to **www.philipallan.co.uk** to see our range of core texts and revision guides.